I0130949

Roots of Revolution

The Press and Social Change in Latin America

Jerry W. Knudson

UNIVERSITY PRESS OF AMERICA,® INC.
Lanham • Boulder • New York • Toronto • Plymouth, UK

Copyright © 2010 by
University Press of America,® Inc.
4501 Forbes Boulevard
Suite 200
Lanham, Maryland 20706
UPA Acquisitions Department (301) 459-3366

Estover Road
Plymouth PL6 7PY
United Kingdom

All rights reserved
British Library Cataloging in Publication Information Available

Library of Congress Control Number: 2009933240
ISBN: 978-0-7618-4822-6 (clothbound : alk. paper)
ISBN: 978-0-7618-4823-3 (paperback : alk. paper)
eISBN: 978-0-7618-4824-0

For Heather

Contents

Acknowledgment

In memory of
C. Alan Hutchison
Professor of Latin American History
University of Virginia

And in gratitude to
Thomas H. Whitehead
Head Special Collections Department
Samuel S. Paley Library
Temple University

Introduction

Anyone questioning the blanket application of North American standards of freedom of the press to Latin America is likely to strike a raw nerve in the body politic of many United States editorial writers and professional organizations. The Inter-American Press Association (IAPA), composed mainly of hemispheric publishers, formed in 1926 and reorganized in 1950, and the Freedom House annual survey, "A Global Survey of Media Independence," which covers 192 countries, may curb some abuses of the press by authoritarian regimes, but in other instances "freedom of the press" may simply cloak the self-interest of class newspaper owners.[1]

Electronic media aside, we tend to forget that as far as the print medium is concerned, the issue of freedom of the press in Latin America ignores several basic facts. Although the situation varies from country to country and statistics are not reliable in the thirty-some Latin American and Caribbean countries, estimates of illiteracy in the region vary from 50 to 80 percent, while others have claimed that half of all Latin Americans have never seen a newspaper.[2]

What then does "freedom of the press" mean to these people, many locked in their isolation for centuries? Radio, of course, bypasses illiteracy, but unfortunately most of the stations play only music, rather than also fulfilling the educational or social possibilities of the medium.

Given the diverse national, ethnic, cultural, linguistic and other variables of the nations studied, it seems apparent that the concept of press freedom in Western industrial democracies, with three or four centuries of give-and-take between government and press, out of which emerged our concept of press freedom, may be inappropriate in other cultures. In Mexico alone, for example, more than 50 Indian languages are spoken (languages, not dialects).

Can—or should—our system be grafted wholly or in part on emerging Third World countries?

It is not denied that many abuses against the press have marred the history of Latin America. Means of government control of the press have included prior censorship, increasingly rare because of the adverse international publicity, confiscation of newspaper or magazine issues after they hit the streets, expropriation of newspapers, radio and television stations (with or without compensation), ceilings on advertisement fees or the sale price of the publications themselves, fomenting labor unrest followed by government intervention, control of newsprint and the latest—and most insidious—the phenomenon of *autocensura* (self-censorship) after a veiled threat by a government official on the telephone, or simply a hint dropped over a cup of coffee as to how a regime wants the news played. More than several Latin American editors have told me they prefer formal censorship during times of civil or international strife, where the boundaries are known, rather than the murky area of self-censorship where journalists may needlessly withhold news.[3]

Various countries have sought their own ways to bring the metropolitan class press closer to the people, such as the Peruvian press law of 1974, which nationalized the eight major newspapers and divided them among various sectors of society, such as the campesinos (Indians), teachers, labor, and so forth, with no governmental control once the transfer was effected. Two, *Expreso* and *Extra*, remained cooperatives, but the proposed system collapsed when the reform military led by General Juan Velasco Alvarado was overthrown in 1980, and the newspapers were returned to their owners.[4]

We exalt freedom of the press in the United States, and rightly so, but we seem intent on forcing our version of government-press relations on other countries. Max Lerner in *America as a Civilization* noted that most of the European press is explicitly political, while that of the United States is implicitly political.[5]

When I first traveled to Denmark in 1979, for example, and asked at a kiosk for a copy of every daily newspaper in Copenhagen, I was astonished when the vendor forked over eleven tabloid-size papers, most representing the views of individual political parties. This was reminiscent of the vigorous partisan press from Jefferson to Jackson in early America. One knew whose viewpoint he was reading, and different viewpoints gave way to more newspapers, a phenomenon which so dazzled Alexis de Toqueville on his visit to America in 1831–32. And William E. Ames, in his careful study of *The National Intelligencer*, regarded as Jefferson's official newspaper, "political journalism, rather than being the dark ages of the American newspaper [a phrase coined by Frank Luther Mott], offered a higher quality of information and interpretation of American society than at any other time in American history."[6]

There were eleven choices in Copenhagen. Philadelphia, with about the same population as all of Denmark, now has only one paper and a tabloid satellite. It is obvious that the acceleration of consolidation of the press in the United States today—Rupert Murdoch's acquisition of the *Wall Street Journal* being the latest example—constricts even further Thomas Jefferson's concept of the "marketplace of ideas."[7] Freedom of the press for whom?

The same is true in Latin America where metropolitan or class newspapers do not penetrate the countryside or shantytowns which ring every major city in the region. The established press has made little or no effort to reach out to these illiterate and poverty-stricken *incomunicados* (those beyond the pale of communication).

Urban class newspapers have for a century or more been dominated by the most prestigious and powerful clans in Latin America—the Gainza Paz family in Argentina, the Agustin Edwards family in Chile, the Miró Quesada and Beltrán families in Peru, and others. Some prestigious newspapers, such as *La Prensa* of Argentina, while extolling "freedom of the press" at international conferences, looked the other way while the military (1976–1983) carried out political genocide that took the lives of 20,000 to 30,000 Argentines during the "dirty war" of 1976–1983.[8]

Thus, the Latin American class press is not always that which is portrayed as benevolent and besieged by malevolent regimes. In the Mexican Revolution which began in 1910, the first social and economic revolution of the twentieth century, seven years before the Bolshevik upheaval in Russia, Francisco Madero, a 19th century liberal who believed that political freedoms would solve all problems, was freely elected President after convulsive fighting, which in all claimed some one million lives. He allowed complete freedom of the press in a country teetering on the brink of counter-revolution. But conservative or reactionary newspapers in Mexico City, hold-overs from the 35-year dictatorship of Porfirio Diaz, undermined the fragile democratic Madero government, making it appear weak and vulnerable, leading to his overthrow and murder, and plunging Mexico into four more years of bloodshed.[9]

Or, to cite a more recent instance, the conservative Chilean press, supported by the CIA, according to a Senate committee headed by Frank Church (D-Idaho) in 1975 and corroborated by principal participants, saturated with adverse propaganda the duly elected Socialist government of Marxist Salvador Allende (1970–1973), setting the stage for the violent overthrow of his government. The result was the seventeen-year backlash of dictator General Augusto Pinochet (1973–1990), one of the harshest regimes in Latin American history.[10]

There was complete freedom of the press under Allende, much to his detriment. (Pinochet died under house arrest in 2007, too ill to face trial on charges of crimes against humanity and corruption). Scholar Patricia Fagen has noted there was a fundamental contradiction in the Allende social revolution: "The supporters of the government sought to employ the forms and even the substance of the mass communication system of the old order in their efforts to create new values."[11]

In Bolivia, on the other hand, under military rule (1964–1980) or Chile under General Augusto Pinochet (1973–1990), journalists faced coercion, harassment, imprisonment, torture or even death. But in a study of the intervention by the IAPA in the Bolivian National Revolution (1952–1964), I found the organization more interested in protecting property rights rather than human rights, including those of reporters. The Committee to Protect Journalists stepped into the breach, ably supported by such human rights groups as Americas Watch and Amnesty International.[12]

Nationalist sentiment is very strong in Latin America—pride in their countries is about all some of them have—and many nationals from all walks of life resent the paternalistic intrusion of the IAPA in the internal affairs of their countries—even though investigating committees are usually composed of both a mixture of American and Latin American publishers or news executives. When I last enquired, the annual membership fee in the IAPA was $500, prohibitive

for most Latin American working journalists, so the voice of labor was never heard in the halls of the IAPA.

When Allende was awaiting the Chilean Congress' final decision on his election the IAPA considered sending an investigating team to see if freedom of the press was threatened in Chile. Apparently, those who advocated such a mission—even before Allende was finally elected—did not know of the great respect for law in Chile, which was then one of the most stable and sophisticated democracies in Latin America before it became a battleground in the Cold War. Chileans were offended by the IAPA proposal. Germán Pico Caños, president of the National Association of the Chilean Pess, made up of owners of Chilean publications, declared at the time that the IAPA, "Is an organism that has become antiquated, and if it does not revise itself to give it greater flexibility, I believe that it will be a very short time until it has no role to play in the future."[13] Even the conservative *El Mercurio* opposed the mission, saying Chileans were best qualified to manage Chilean affairs.

One of the most encouraging signs of recent years has been the spreading professionalization of journalists in associations, neither union nor guild, but parts of both, known as *colegios*. Although requirements for membership vary from country to country, usually one must have a university degree in Journalism (called Schools of Social Communication) or equivalent experience in order to practice journalism. This not only raises salaries by restricting the labor market (Journalists in Latin America frequently must hold down two or even three jobs to make ends meet) and pitifully low salaries in their media jobs make them vulnerable to bribes or the enticement of radical politics. Critics of the *colegio* system cry "Licensing!" but the government has no connection with the *colegios*, which also take active roles in causes affecting them, such as infringements on freedom of the press, or access to government information. Thus, proponents maintain *colegios* are no different than the American Bar Association or American Medical Association, both of which set their own standards with no governmental control. By 1993, journalists had formed national *colegios* in thirteen Latin American republics despite strong opposition from press owners.[14]

Thus, Latin America itself has come up with a way toward a more equitable press system which fits their needs and is consonant with their values. They ask not only freedom *from* what but also freedom *for* what. Among the English language surveys, I prefer that of Freedom House, which embraces a broadly based concept of "independence" rather than "freedom of the press," which tolerates different systems which allow constructive roles for all.

NOTES

1. Jerry W. Knudson, "Freedom of the Press in Latin America: Another View." *Studies in Latin American Popular Culture*, Vol. 2 (1983) 239–243.

2. Jon Vanden Heuvel and Everette E. Dennis, *Changing Patterns, Latin America's Vital Media*, "A Report of the Freedom Forum Media Studies Center" (New York: Columbia University, 1995). For radio and television. See page 56.

3. Jerry Knudson, "Self-Censorship in the Venezuelan Press," *The Times of the Americas* (February 22, 1989), page 10.

4. Jerry Knudson, "The Peruvian Press Law of 1974: The Other Side of the Coin," *Mass. Comm. Review*, Vol. 5, No. 2 (Spring 1978).

5. Max Lerner, *America as a Civilization*.

6. William R. Ames, *A History of the National Intelligencer* (Chapel Hill: University of North Carolina Press, 1972).

7. Jerry W. Knudson, *Jefferson and the Press, Crucible of Liberty* (Columbia, SC: University of South Carolina Press, 2006), 165–174.

8. Jerry Knudson, "Veil of Silence, The Argentine Press and the 'Dirty War,' 1976–1983," *Latin American Perspectives,* Vol. 24, No. 6 (September 1997), 93–112.

9. Jerry W. Knudson, "John Reed, A Reporter in Revolutionary Mexico," *Journalism History*, Vol. 29, No. 2 (Summer 2003), 59–68.

10. Jerry W. Knudson, *The Chilean Press During the Allende Years, 1970–73.* (Buffalo: State University of New York at Buffalo, 1986) Special Studies Publications, 152.

11. Patricia Fagen, "The Media in Allende's Chile," *Journal of Communication* (Winter 1974), 63–64. See also, Jerry W. Knudson, "A Selected Bibliography of the Chilean Press During the Allende and Pinochet Years," *International Communication Bulletin*, Vol. 42, No. 1–2 (Spring 2007), 53–56.

12. Jerry W. Knudson, *Bolivia: Press and Revolution, 1932–1964* (Lanham, MD: University Press of America, 1986).

13. *La Nación*, November 5, 1971.

14. Jerry W. Knudson, "Licensing Journalists in Latin America: An Appraisal," *Journalism and Mass Communications Quarterly*, Vol. 73, No. 4 (Winter 1996), 878–889.

Chapter One

The Mexican Revolution of 1910

PRELUDE TO A TROUBLED CENTURY

Americans tend not to understand social and economic revolutions because their own historical experience after 1776 was largely political. When fighting broke out all over Mexico in 1910, most news accounts in the United States viewed it as simply another exuberant Latin American coup d'etat, this one to rid Mexico of the 35-year dictatorship of Porfirio Diaz. Francisco I. Madero, a wealthy landowner in the north, elected President in 1910, in some respects the political figurehead of the Mexican Revolution, believed that political freedoms would solve everything once his election was honored. But the unfolding drama brought to the forefront centuries of grievances which spilled over into seven years of armed conflict, numerous protagonists, and one million dead, including the influenza epidemic of 1917.

Porfirio Diaz sought to modernize Mexico by granting foreign firms and individuals almost anything they wanted. William Randolph Hearst, for example, acquired huge chunks of northern Mexico for his cattle ranches. Profits from industry, railroads, oil—all were repatriated profits, which led to a folk saying, "Mexico is the mother of foreigners and the step-mother of Mexicans."

When exactly did Francisco I. Madero, denied the election of 1910 rightly his, decide on revolution by issuing his Plan of San Luis Potosi, which made only a vague promise of land reform, carried out by legal means? Although not clearly recognized by all at the time, agrarian adjustment—land redistribution—was the cause that tore a nation apart. In this sense, Madero, a dedicated democrat who believed that political freedoms would solve everything, unleashed forces beyond his control. Early biographers insisted that Madero never intended revolution, but a letter from him to William Randolph Hearst,

1

responding to written questions submitted to him by the New York publisher, clearly stated, "I knew that General Diaz could only be defeated by means of arms but the democratic [electoral] campaign [of 1910] was indispensable because this would prepare public opinion and justify the armed uprising." (I discovered this letter in the Biblioteca Nacional in Mexico City, and it was published in full in *The Americas*, 30:6 (1974). The portion quoted here is from page 329.)

WORDS THAT IGNITED A REVOLUTION

In the tightly controlled society of Porfirian Mexico, dissident voices were rare, but those who managed to get through thus carried more weight. One was an unwitting handmaiden to revolution. An article by James Creelman in *Pearson's Magazine*, "President Diaz, Hero of the Americas," 19:3 (March 1908), 231–277, while generally laudatory of Diaz, also quoted him as saying, "No matter what my friends and supporters say, I retire when my present term of office ends, and I shall not serve again. I shall be eighty years old then (p. 242)." Obviously intended for foreign consumption, the article was translated into Spanish and was circulated clandestinely in Mexico. This was the opening Francisco Madero had been waiting for.

In 1963, the Mexican government considered this article so pivotal in opening the flood-gates of revolution that it authorized a facsimile edition of the entire piece, along with Spanish translation, by the Universidad Nacional Autonoma de Mexico.

Francisco Madero published *The Presidential Succession of 1910* in 1908. His book underwent three significant editions. At first, Madero opted for the vice-presidential slot, assuming that Diaz would die before completing his eighth term. But Madero became more assertive after the Creelman interview and came out boldly through his newspaper *La Nueva Era* for the presidency itself under the slogan, "Effective Suffrage, No Re-Election."

Other voices were also striving to be heard. Andres Molina Enriquez brought forth a book in 1909, *Los Grandes problemas nacionales*, which was the first to pinpoint the Mexican crisis on the unjust distribution of land, coupled with a burgeoning population. This book, suppressed by the Diaz regime, but not until many copies had been distributed, laid down the gauntlet. Land reform would come, he wrote, "whether in peace . . . or revolution."

Other voices of dissent were also heard. Foremost among them was Ricardo Flores Magon, his brother and others, who launched the anarchist newspaper, *Regeneracion*. Barred from Mexico, *Regeneracion* continued to be published in San Antonio and Los Angeles and was distributed clandestinely in pre-

Revolutionary Mexico. The influence of this newspaper can be measured when Guttierez de Lara, a Mexican congressman, visited Los Angeles in August 1910 and declared, "I know that Diaz fears the publication of this paper [*Regeneracion*] more than a thousand armed revolutionaries." (*New York Times*, August 19, 1910). Flores Magon, pursued and finally captured by U.S. and Mexican agents, died in Leavenworth prison in Kansas, never seeing the revolution he had helped foment. (See Marc Tarry Killinger, "An Assessment of the Coverage of Ricardo Flores Magon and *Regeneracion* in the *New York Times* 1900–1924," unpublished manuscript, Temple University, 1990.)

The contradiction between Madero's idealism and the raw reality of those hungry for power, together with a hostile Mexico City press that made him seem weak and vulnerable, led to his overthrow and murder in 1913 in a counter-revolution led by General Victoriano Huerta. This plunged Mexico into four more years of bloodshed that finally saw Venustiano Carranza emerge triumphant, recognized by the United States as the *de facto* government of Mexico. This internecine conflict had been codified in the Constitution of 1917, but it would become reality only much later. Oil was not nationalized until 1937, and substantial land reform awaited the administration of Lazaro Cardenas (1934–1940).

Out of the conflict, however, arose a unique one-party system to guarantee the peace, which after several variations culminated in the Party of the Institutional Revolution (PRI), called by some "the perfect dictatorship" with the outgoing President choosing his successor (*el tapado*, the one tapped on the shoulder). Others claimed the PRI was just as democratic as any primary in the United States since all sectors of Mexican society were represented, such as labor, industrialists, teachers, and so forth. But critics point out that as the years passed, the PRI became a bloated bureaucracy riddled with corruption, and so Mexico once again has become a multi-party system.

Economist Walt Rostow long ago declared that Mexico and Brazil had passed the "take-off" stage of economic development (*The Process of Economic Growth*, 1952) on the road to industrialization. But rapid growth with unregulated factories and industrial plants spewed forth pollutants which prevailing winds trapped between mountain ranges that enfolded the central plateau where Mexico City is located. These wastes from the northern industrial section of the city created smog so dense in the 1950s that at times motorists on the Paseo de la Reforma were compelled to turn on their headlights at high noon.

On the other hand, scholar Frank Tannenbaum of Columbia University (*Ten Keys to Latin America*, 1962) argued that Mexico should remain content with her native culture. Americans may think only Spanish is spoken in Mexico, but actually 52 Indian languages (languages, not dialects) enrich this beautiful country which could be based on tourism and the arts and crafts for which Mexico is famous.

As for the arts which Tannenbaum so cherished, the foremost contribution to world culture of the Mexican Revolution was a revival of mural painting—with political messages brought vividly before the people on the walls of almost every public building, not only in Mexico but also in the United States and elsewhere. Led by the three masters of the genre—Diego Rivera, David Alfaro Siqueiros, and Jose Clemente Orozco—the art historian Jean Charlot has called this explosion of creativity *The Mexican Mural Renaissance, 1920–1925*. In literature, such towering figures as Carlos Fuente and Octavio Paz dazzled the world.

Today, the social and economic Mexican Revolution which began in 1910 and faded out after 1940, remains mostly national mythology and even that is disappearing. In a swank Mexico City night club, I asked the small orchestra if they would play "Adelita," one of the leading *corridos* or ballads of the Mexican Revolution. They did not know it. Instead, they offered "My Adobe Hacienda," straight out of what used to be called Tin Pan Alley. However, later on the same trip, on Cozumel Island, a ragged boy approached me in the plaza with his battered guitar and asked for requests. "Do you know `Adelita' I asked, and his face lit up as he launched into the song, endless verse after verse, which buoyed the spirits of a people during a crucial time in their history. He was still playing and singing, coming up with more and more verses, when I had to leave. But in my mind, he is still cornering tourists and joyfully singing songs of the Mexican Revolution for a few coins.

But do the ballads of that period still resonate in the hearts of men and women who risk life and limb to leave Mexico in search of work in the United States? The population explosion amidst the poverty-stricken rural areas and the destitute shanty-towns which ring every gleaming metropolitan center in Latin America, impelled thousands and thousands of Mexicans to seek work illegally in the United States.

Their plight was exacerbated by the terms of the North Atlantic Free Trade Agreement (NAFTA) which overlooked the human cost of "modernizing" Mexico. NAFTA's threat to the ancient *ejidos* or communal lands in Chiapas, the southernmost and most impoverished Mexican state, ignited a rebellion that initially cost more than one hundred lives and ended in a stalemate.

Perhaps the plight of these disinherited is best exemplified in the work of Alejandro Santiago, a Mexican sculptor who, upon returning from Paris, found his native village of Teococuilco deserted except for children and the old folks. The men of the village had all gone north in search of work and money to send back home to their destitute families. The sculptor Santiago decided to repopulate his town with 2,501 statues, each measuring four feet and six inches tall, as an artistic protest. With a grant of $100,000 from the Rockefeller Foundation to pay the 35 artisans who completed the task, the statues are mute witnesses to the death of a Mexican village and to commemorate all those who lost their lives attempting to cross the United States border in search of jobs and money to be sent back home to their families. To accommodate immigrants, Mexico increased the number of its consulates in the United States to 49. (Washington Post, August 6, 2007).

Among the outstanding issues facing the new President, Felipe Calderon, was legislation signed by President George W. Bush a year earlier authorizing 700 miles of fencing along the 2,000 mile border between the United States and Mexico. Mexican Ambassador to the United States Sarukhan declared, "We do consider in a respectful way that it would be better to stop the migration by building a kilometer of highway in Michoacan or Zacatecas than 10 kilometers of walls in the border." (Washington Post, March 23, 2007).

Another serious problem was the violence in Mexico by rival drug cartels, although most observers fail to point out that these cartels would not exist if those in the United States would not buy their illegal smuggled drugs. Mexico is not entirely to blame, and with assistance from the United States, President Calderon is vigorously attacking the problem. (Washington Post, August 6, 2007).

JOHN REED: RIDING WITH PANCHO VILLA

In some respects, the Twentieth Century did not begin in 1900 but rather in 1910 with the outbreak of the Mexican revolution, which was to last almost a decade and cost 1,000,000 lives. It preceded the Bolshevik upheaval in Russia by seven years when Marxist-Leninist theory was put to the test at the barricades in 1917. Both events ushered in a century riddled with global and nationalistic wars. It was truly the revolutionary century, bridged in the first decades by John Reed, a young reporter from Portland, Oregon, who not only rode with the forces of Pancho Villa in the Mexican Revolution but later wrote an eye-witness account of the Russian Revolution which became a classic of modern journalism, *Ten Days that Shook the World*.

Unfortunately for Reed, however, his Mexican dispatches—some of which were collected in 1914 as *Insurgent Mexico*—were later over-shadowed by the world's attention focused on Russia. Reed's graphic reportage from Mexico has gone largely unnoticed, although it proved his writing prowess. The only reference to Reed in Mexico in Warren Beatty's motion picture *Reds* is a shot of Villa charging his troops on horseback across the opening credits. The film itself was essentially a love story between Reed and Louise

Bryant. A Mexican movie, *Reed: Mexico Insurgente*, which was directed by Paul Leduc and based faithfully on Reed's book, somewhat righted the scales, but the film was not widely distributed.

Seven biographies of John Reed have appeared. All have been consulted for this work, and most include a chapter on Mexico. But almost without exception they concentrate on Reed's relationship with Villa and his coming of age under fire. Few dwell on his contributions to journalism while in Mexico, although many of these biographies provide fascinating contextual details and attest to his overall significance. It is this meager attention to his reporting of the Mexican revolution that this article seeks to redress from the historical perspective.

The primary sources are about 100 pages of the handwritten Mexican notebook of Reed along with thirty boxes of material, all of which are available at the Houghton Library of Harvard University. Only a few scholars have skimmed the notebook because it is disorganized and parts are scarcely legible. Yet it is well worth deciphering, for Reed's jottings, sometimes under fire, are the raw material of great reporting. This article also is based on everything he published on the Mexican revolution in the United States, from what appeared in radical journals to mainstream newspapers, as identified by specialists at the Library of Congress. The author has studied all of the original print sources rather than accounts of them because some dispatches were omitted and others altered in Reed's compilation of 1914, *Insurgent Mexico*.

Four months after arriving in Mexico in December 1913, Reed was a conduit of information, accurate or embellished, about Mexico for readers in the United States.

Historians would be remiss to dismiss his work because it was literary—even poetic—and at times seemed to stretch the truth to offer the essence of an event or personality to readers unfamiliar with Mexican culture. While Reed eschewed what others called "objectivity," historians are increasingly beginning to realize that newspapers or journal articles in a sense are primary documents in the formation of public opinion if people read and believe the information available to them, which may condition their subsequent actions.

Reed was a forerunner of the 1960s "New Journalism," which is still around under the rubric of "Literary Journalism" and is news reporting with greater evocative techniques to compete with the visual and immediate impact of television. The term New Journalism has been bandied about ever since it was applied to Joseph Pulitzer's emphasis on sensational human interest stories in the 1880s, which were designed to lure readers onto the editorial page. Some have even traced it as far back as the novelists of the early nineteenth century. John C. Hartsock has brought this up to date with his landmark study, *A History of American Literary Journalism,* in which he stated, "But if the first major period of narrative literary journalism had passed, the form was still practiced and published during the [1910s and 1920s.]" He included Reed in the group doing this type of writing, and a sample of his writing will show why.

For example, as the military phase of the Mexican revolution unfolded, Reed wrote in the aftermath of one battle: "The shooting never ceased, but it seemed to be subdued to its subordinate place in a fantastic and disordered world. Up the [railroad] track in the hot morning light straggled a river of wounded men, shattered, bleeding, bound up in rotting and bloody bandages, inconceivably weary."

Despite recent neglect, Reed was appreciated in liberal circles in his own time. As Walter Lippmann wrote, "If all history had been reported as you are doing this, Lord! I say with Jack Reed reporting begins." He also wrote Reed, "Your first two articles [in *Metropolitan*] are undoubtedly the finest reporting that's ever been [done]." The young journalist also was praised by contemporaries such as Rudyard Kipling, who said, "His articles in the *Metropolitan* made me see Mexico," and John Dos Passos. Reed's work also was compared to that of Richard Harding Davis and Stephen Crane. Eugene Debs, the Socialist candidate for President four times who amassed 901,000 votes in 1912, wrote Reed, "You write differently than anyone else and your style is most appealing to me. There is something that breathes and throbs in all you say."

Reed, who later formed the forerunner of the American Communist Party, was not unaware of the power of the written word in the time before radio and television. As Edgcumb Pinchon, the first credible biographer of the southern agrarian reform fighter Emiliano Zapata, wrote to Reed, "The great mass, as you say, only can be stirred by the direct appeal to the emotions; and by George, we have to take that fact into our reckoning at every turn, if we are to get anywhere."

Actually, there was an early connection between Villa, with whom Reed hooked up, and Emiliano Zapata, revered southern guerilla fighter. Reed included in his papers a safe-conduct pass for Maximo Castillo, seeking a union between the forces of the two men, who were to meet later briefly in Mexico City.

As one who became a dedicated Communist, Reed could write passion-ately with conviction, but outside radical circles, he was still at the bottom of the American cultural heap. As John Stuart, editor of one of the collections of Reed's writings pointed out: "Here by wide acknowledgment was a great American journalist, an eyewitness to the greatest story of the time, but not an editor outside the tiny radical press would give him an inch of space."

This, however, is not entirely accurate. Before he went to Mexico in December 1913, Reed, who previously had published only short stories and poetry, sought to shore up his reportorial credentials by getting an assignment from a mainstream newspaper. He had left his position as sub-editor of *American Magazine*, which had been launched by renegade writers from S.S. McClure's publication, to direct a labor pageant, but he had no real newspaper writing experience. The *New York Sun*, launched as a penny paper in 1833, turned him down, but the *New York World*, which had been bought by Pulitzer in 1882, took Reed on and the young journalist did at least six lengthy stories on the Mexican revolution for the *World*. Biographer David C. Duke, without citing his source, wrote: "Apparently Reed had little enthusiasm for the work he did for the *World*. It was almost an afterthought, halfheartedly done, for the purpose of earning a little extra money." On the contrary, Reed was intent on bringing the truth about the Mexican revolution home to his American readers. He realized that the *World* was a better vehicle to do this than the small-circulation radical publications for which he also wrote, such as the *Metropolitan* and *The Masses*.

At any rate, sympathy for the Mexican revolutionary cause was perhaps the result of his youth and education in the broader sense. He was not a rebel from the outset—declining to join the Socialist Club founded by Lippmann at Harvard—but his experiences in a Patterson, New Jersey, textile strike politicized him. As a free-lance writer, he was jailed for twenty days but was released after only four days (at his arraignment, the magistrate asked Reed his profession and he replied, "Poet.") Ironically, the Patterson strike, one of the longest in American history, was fought by workers who wove United States flags. To justify bringing in non-union workers, the mill owners proclaimed, "We live under the flag; we fight for this flag; and we will work under this flag." Demonstrators countered with the slogan, "We wove the flag; we dyed the flag; we won't scab under the flag." Reed was so moved by the plight of the laborers at Paterson that he organized a proletarian pageant or street theater at the Old Madison Square Garden in New York with a cast of almost 1,000 workers brought in from the strike area who performed before an audience of 20,000. An artistic success, the pageant failed to raise money for the strikers, but Reed was molded by the experience. In retrospect, Lippmann lamented, "Even as an undergraduate he betrayed what many people believe to be the central passion of his life, an inordinate desire to be arrested."

Reed was born in Portland, Oregon, in 1887 into a prominent family that later suffered business reverses. His grandfather had amassed a fortune in the early lumber business, and his father evidenced a social conscience as a U.S. marshal appointed by Theodore Roosevelt. Together with Lincoln Steffens and others, John's father smashed the Oregon Land Fraud Ring, a brave undertaking in the state at the time, but failed to be elected to the United States Senate by a narrow margin. At great personal sacrifice, his father later sent his two sons through Harvard.

Reed, introspective as most writers, began writing his autobiography at the age of thirty; it was never completed, and the fragment was not published until 1936. It is this insight into his own youth which is presented here. As a boy, he was not in good health until a kidney was removed at sixteen. He described himself as a coward, when confronted by the bullies of Portland, until he began to find a place for himself at the Morristown School in New Jersey. But throughout his youth, he wrote, "history was my passion, kings strutting about and the armored ranks of men-at-arms clashing forward in close ranks against a hail of cloth-yard shafts."

His class consciousness was sharpened at Harvard where he was shunned as an upstart Westerner by sons of the Back Bay Brahmins. He wrote for campus publications, became a cheerleader, and was elected president of the Cosmopolitan Club, which then had members of forty-three nationalities. After graduation, Reed worked his way to Europe on a cattle boat. He could have afforded passage but preferred to experience the life of a common laborer. Returning from a year of tramping around Europe, he settled in Greenwich Village and soaked up the life of New York. As he wrote in "Almost Thirty," which was published in the *New Republic* after his death, "In New York I first loved, and I first wrote of the things I saw, with a fierce joy of creation—and knew at last that I could write." The class chasms of New York also polarized Reed, as when he wrote: "I couldn't help but observe the ugliness of poverty and all its train of evil, the cruel inequality tween [sic] rich people who had too many motor cars and poor people, who didn't have enough to eat. It didn't come to me from books that the workers produced all the wealth of the world, which went to those who did not earn it."

Chafing at the bit, Reed turned to small liberal publications to vent his indignation. At first, it was *The Masses* where his work originally appeared in January 1913 and where he served as managing editor under Max Eastman. He wholeheartedly subscribed to the publication's creed: "The broad Purpose of *The Masses* is a social one: to everlastingly attack old systems, old morals, old prejudices—the whole weight of outworn thought that dead men have saddled upon us—and to set up new ones in their places."

At this point, Mexico reeled under a counter-revolution. The primordial reason for it was hunger for land. When fighting had begun in 1910, bringing an end to the thirty-five year dictatorship of Porfirio Diaz, land was concentrated in 4,944 haciendas or large estates while the country was importing foodstuffs. Ownership of land was regarded for its social prestige rather than productive value. Moreover, the Mexican Catholic Church, it was said,

owned half of the national territory through inalienable bequests. Reed was
quick to point this out in an article for *The Masses*: "In the first place, [the
Mexican revolution] is not a revolution of the middle class; it is a slowly-
growing accumulation of grievances of the peons—lowest class—which has
finally burst definitely into expression. There is not one peon out of twenty
who cannot tell you exactly what they are all fighting for: Land." The most
spectacular example of land aggrandizement occurred in Chihuahua where
the Terrazas family owned 17 million acres of land (three-fourths of the state)
in addition to their business enterprises.

Twenty-six-year-old Reed followed events south of the Rio Grande
closely. When the fighting stopped and Diaz was forced into exile in 1911,
Francisco Madero, son of a wealthy landowner in the North and a political
figurehead of the revolution, was elected president. It seemed the rebellion
was over. Reed was incensed, however, when in 1913 General Victoriano
Huerta staged a bloody counter-revolution in Mexico City, murdered Madero
and vice-president Pino Suarez, and plunged the country into civil war. Opposition to Huerta came from Villa in the northwest, Venustiano Carranza in
the northeast, and Zapata in the south.

When Huerta attacked the democratic government of Madero, Carl
Hovey, editor of the *Metropolitan*, cast about for a correspondent to send
there. The *New York Tribune* had fielded Davis, and others flocked to the
scene (many, according to Reed, getting no closer to Mexico than the bars
of El Paso). With war approaching in Europe, numerous American expatri-
ates fled south of the border, including Ambrose Bierce (who disappeared
and was presumed executed after a falling out with Villa), Katharine Anne
Porter, Hart Crane, and Steffens. Upon the advice of the latter, Hovey made
an offer to Reed, who gladly accepted, and the adventure of his lifetime was
about to begin.

After his paramour Mabel Dodge became bored with life in El Paso and
soon returned to New York, Reed went into Mexico alone. Not beholden to
anyone, he waded across the torpid Rio Grande, noting in his memoir, "When
I first crossed the border deadliest fear gripped me. I was afraid of death, of
mutilation, of a strange land and strange people whose speech and thought
I did not know." Nevertheless, he sent several letters before filing formal
dispatches to Hovey, who printed them with the admonition, "Although not
intended for publication, these pen pictures are too vivid to be lost." The letters included this description, referring to the forces of Villa, the chieftain of
the north with whom Reed hooked up:

> They [Villa's soldiers] formed in fours, and at the sound of a cracked bugle
> they loosened their reins, lashed with their quirts, leaned over and yelled in the
> horses' ears, and burst into a wild charge like a clap of thunder. I never saw

anything like it. Two thousand nondescript, tattered men, on dirty little tough horses, their serapes flying out behind, their mouths one wild yell, simply flung themselves out over the plain.

Reed sought an interview with General Salvador Mercado, who headed the Federal or counter-revolutionary forces in the north that sought to undo the democratic promise of the Madero presidency. But the young journalist's note fell into the hands of Pascual Orozco, a renegade general who defected from Madero's cause. Orozco warned Reed: "Esteemed and honored Sir: If you set foot in Ojinaga [a town then being contested] I will stand you sideways against a wall, and with my own hand take great pleasure in shooting furrows in your back." Reed ignored the note but waited to enter Ojinaga with Villa's troops.

The first encounter between Reed and Villa was heralded in the lead headline of the *New York World* on March 1, 1914: "Villa Is Brutal, Yet He Has Ideals, *World* Man Finds." The meeting took place in El Paso on February 27. Reed found "A stout, heavy Mexican, with a mustache, dressed in a soiled brown suit, his shirt collar open at the throat [who] was kicking mules" aboard the railway freight cars for the advance on Torreon. It is difficult to separate Villa the man from Pancho Villa the legend. He became an outlaw and a folk hero after killing a Federal soldier for allegedly raping his sister. Fleeing to the mountains of Durango, he spent twenty-two years as a bandit rustling cattle from rich *hacendados* until the Revolution gave him a place in the scheme of things. A staunch supporter of Madero, who spearheaded the drive against the dictator Diaz, he racked up a series of impressive battles in the north of Mexico, which attracted Reed to his ranks.

Reed had yet to experience battle. On January 14, 1914, Villa's small band of 100 Indians, known as La Tropa, finally captured Ojinaga, which had changed hands five times in the course of fighting and was little more than a pile of rubble. The journalist had his foot in the door by establishing contact with Villa's forces. Both men seemed fascinated with each other, so much so that Villa issued a pass ordering civil and military authorities to give Reed aid and protection. He would also be allowed to use railway and telegraph lines without charge.

At first, Reed was not fully accepted by La Tropa, with whom he rode whenever a horse was available. After a night of carousing in an abandoned and looted hacienda building, an irate Mexican cried, "We want no correspondents. We want no words printed in a book. We want rifles and killing, and if we die, we will be caught up among the saints!" A friend of Reed's, Longinos Guereca, intervened in the dispute, saying: "That's enough! Julian Reyes, you know nothing. This *compañero* comes thousands of miles by the sea and the land to tell his countrymen the truth of the fight for liberty. He goes into battle without any arms; he's braver than you are, because you have a rifle. Get out now and don't bother him any more!"

During the campaign for northern Mexico, transportation was always a problem. Reed requested a horse so he could ride in the vanguard of La Tropa, but Villa replied, "Listen, Senor Reporter, do you know that about a thousand men in my army have no horses? What do you want a horse for? Here's the train." In fact, the Revolution in large part was fought using the railways, particularly in the arid or semi-arid north where vast distances slowed military operations. When the Constitutionalist army opposing the usurper Huerta split into factions headed by Villa in the northwest and Álvaro Obregon in the northeast, Carranza, First Chief of the Constitutionalist army, deliberately cut off the supply of coal to Villa's twelve trains so that his man, Obregon, could reach Mexico City first. Thus, the revolution continued to be a power struggle.

Reed noted that atop the railroad box-cars "the cooking fires of the *soldaderas* [women who fought] flared from the freight cars." Every square foot of space was crowded with people to make room for the flatbed cannons, artillery caissons, and machine guns. It should also be noted that for the first time in Mexican history, there was a field hospital—a separate train—to care for the wounded. When the enemy temporarily destroyed the tracks ahead, life was doubly harsh. As Reed reported, "No one had anything to eat. The night came on cold and few had blankets. Hundreds of women camp followers were rushing aimlessly around crying for their men." Even with the trains, it took four days of hard riding to the nearest telegraph station before the news could be flashed to a waiting world.

Reed experienced his first combat at the hacienda of La Cadena, garrisoned by 150 *villista* soldiers. Routed by overwhelming Federal forces, Reed and others ran pell-mell into the desert. Shedding his camera and jacket, the journalist found refuge at a friendly hacienda and noted, "Well, this is certainly an experience. I'm going to have something to write about." He also pointed out, "It is almost impossible to get objective about the desert; you sink into it—become a part of it." As for the surrounding mountain range, he felt it was "wrinkled like a giant's bedclothes."

At last, Reed began to make a name for himself. The first of the La Tropa articles appeared in the *Metropolitan* in April 1914 along with large advertisements in newspapers promoting the series. *World* delivery trucks also emblazoned on their sides praise for his Mexican reporting. Later, Hovey, the editor of *Metropolitan*, cabled Reed, "Battle article received. Nothing finer could have been written. You are sending us great stuff."

Yet Reed was always anxious about his work and open to criticism, whether sending copies for review to Charles Townsend Copeland, his former Harvard professor of composition, and admonishing Hovey, "I think the thing will stand stronger just in raw colors. Please go through it carefully, and where I have slopped over, edit mercilessly." He kept a shorthand book of his Mexican observations. While it is not often cited by researchers because of its illegible or jumbled prose, it is well worth disentangling as it reveals the journalist in action. For example, Reed's impressions of a battle and its aftermath were recorded as: "Big guns booming like bells. Hellish chatter of musketry fire. Woodpecker stabs of machine guns . . . Fires with bloody men around them. Dead bodies. Wounded straggling back."

Perhaps because of this nightmarish milieu, Reed drew closer to his fighting companions and the Mexican people in general. He "squatted around the fire of cactus roots, and greasewood [with them], cooking their eternal frijoles and tortillas." He rode with them all day and drank and danced all night, usually in looted hacienda buildings. He wrote in his autobiographical fragment, "I made good with these wild fighting men, and with myself. I loved them and I loved the life. I found myself again. I wrote better than I have ever written."

In contrast, Reed had nothing but contempt for the American soldiers of fortune who generally fought with the Federales, declaring, "Soon I left [a small group of] them, hard, cold misfits in a passionate country, despising the cause for which they were fighting, sneering at the gaiety of the irrepressible Mexicans." As for the Mexicans themselves, Reed wrote, "There are no people whom I have seen who are so close to nature as these people are. They are just like their mud houses, just like their little crops of corn." He also noted that the revolution enveloped everyone. For example, there was seven-year-old Manuel Martinez, who fought with the Madero forces. And there were unspeakable atrocities, such as after the battle of Tierra Blanca, when it was said that a *villista* officer named Torielo shot forty-five prisoners, pausing only to load every few minutes.

Reed came to idolize Villa, admiring his swift, forced charges of calvary, coupled with surprise night attacks. They faced the *colorados* or Federal troops, remnants of Orozco's army. One example of Villa's military prowess was the capture of Juárez. He had conquered General Mercado in Chihuahua with 6,000 men. Then at Juárez, across the Rio Grande from El Paso, he slipped around to the railroad station with 1,000 men, captured the operator, and surrounded the town and took it by surprise.

Through it all, Reed had to fight constantly against the cheap stereotypes heaped on the Mexicans by their United States counterparts. Looking back in 1916, he wrote, "When we think of a Mexican, we usually picture, half-derisively, an undersized, treacherous little half-breed fit to kick around on a section gang, but really not worth much." He hooked up with an American in Mexico identified only as Mac, who was a mine foreman whose hatred knew no national bounds. He thought it was "great sport to hunt niggers in Georgia," for instance. Reed summed up the American attitude: "Mexican peons are a shiftless, contented, ambitionless race. They must be kept broke (pay every day) or else they won't work." Mac chimed in, "These people we've got up here [mines of Durango] are the best of the Mexicans. Not like the God damned scum that joins a revolution just for the chance to murder and steal." This bigotry was not limited to Americans in Mexico. In fact, Americans had insisted before Reed went to Mexico that the Mexican was "fundamentally dishonest." This found its way into the mainstream press of the United States. On January 12, 1912, *Harper's Weekly*, for example, deplored "the slouchiness, the laziness, the stupidity and the cowardliness of the average Mexican."

Thus, Reed faced a gargantuan task in getting his readers to identify with the Mexican people and their aspirations. While recognizing cultural differences, the young American journalist painted word pictures depicting the human side of Mexicans in accounts laced with gentle humor. He delighted in conveying to his readers a typical Mexican patio bursting with life—children two years old and older, mostly naked, holding hens in their laps or riding pigs. And there were the adolescents "up to fourteen or fifteen years old, already swaggering in chaps and revolvers if boys, and flirting with their eyes if girls."

But Reed was not blind to one fault of his hosts. "When a Mexican is drunk, there is no accounting for him," he wrote in his notebook. "But when he's sober, courtesy, frankness and honest dealing will enable anybody to get along with him." The theme of generosity occurred time and again in Reed's impressions of Mexicans. "As a matter of fact," he noted, "a Mexican will share with you or anybody his last crust. Generous, impulsive, they will do anything for you if you pour out yourself to them in any way." When a countryman offered Reed shelter in his flight from the defeat at La Cadena, the reporter wrote, "He was like all peons, incredibly poor and lavishly hospitable."

After the capture of Chihuahua, capital of the state of the same name, Villa made a speech from the balcony of the government house proclaiming that he was there to keep order, to protect life and property, and to guarantee business. On November 17, 1910, the nucleus of Villa's "army" had consisted of only fifteen men. After the overthrow and murder of Madero, Villa had taken to the mountains again with only eight men. Now his Division of the North had nine brigades. Not everyone had high hopes for Villa as military governor of Chihuahua, however. Reed was frank in recognizing Villa's limitations: "Villa was the son of ignorant peons. He had never been to school. He hadn't any conception of the complexity of civilization, and when he finally came back to it, a mature man of extraordinary shrewdness, he encountered the twentieth century with the naive simplicity of a savage."

As military governor of Chihuahua, Villa, Reed reported, "began the extraordinary experiment—extraordinary because he knew nothing about it—of creating a government for 400,000 people out of his own head." He issued a proclamation fixing the price of beef at seven cents a pound, milk at five cents a quart, and bread at four cents a loaf. Advised that there was a shortage of money, Villa issued his own with the only guarantee his name printed on the bills. He had social plans for the future once the fighting stopped. He proposed settling his soldiers on cooperatives with sixty-two-and-a-half acres of land for each man; it would be inalienable land for ten years. Moreover, there would be a three-day work week plus one day of military training to protect the land. This may not sound so visionary when one considers the ancient *ejidos* or communal lands of the Mexican villages. Cooperation, not exploitation was the rule.

Such idealistic schemes apparently did not seep down through the ranks of men and women who had a concrete idea why they were fighting, Reed discovered. The reporter asked why a particular man fought and was told, "Why, it is good, fighting. You don't have to work in the mines." Another said, "You get better whiskey." But Policarpo Castro added, with obvious commitment and simplicity, that he fought for land and liberty. But what was meant by liberty? One barefoot peon soldier said, "Liberty is when I can do what I want!" In his notebook Reed quoted Benito Juárez, the Indian president of the late nineteenth century, who declared, "Peace is respect for others' rights." Another man asked if there was war in the United States. When told there was no war, he asked, "How do you pass the time, then?"

There were moments of introspection, however, amidst the drunken carousing as the soldiers unwound after a hard day's battle. Waiting for a night attack, one combatant lamented, "Oh, aren't we brave, we Mexicans killing each other?" Another soldier with a philosophical bent ventured, "I am not an educated man, but I know that to fight is the last resort of any people. Only when things get too bad to stand, eh? And if we are going to kill our brothers something fine must come out of it, eh?"

Having conquered surrounding towns in the North and Chihuahua, Villa braced for the assault on Torreon, gateway to San Luis Potosi and Mexico City. The siege was the highlight of Reed's dispatches from Mexico, although he reported the fall of the city before it actually happened. Meanwhile, with some exaggeration, Reed telegraphed that Villa used 20,000 "bombs" against Torreon, a statement that ended up in a *World* headline. These grenades of dynamite, wrapped in cowhide thrown by galloping cavalrymen, were found to be more useful than rifles in dislodging Federals from behind adobe walls. On their part, the enemy poisoned the irrigation ditches, and many horses and men in the *villista* ranks died.

When the fall of Torreon became imminent, Villa ordered that no news be sent until it occurred. After the decisive five-day battle at Gómez Palacio, which was the threshold to Torreon, Reed rushed to El Paso on March 24, 1914, to flash the news to the outside world even though it was a week before the last of the federal troops had fled Torreon. He noted that the federals had attempted to leave the city twice, but the railway had been torn up by the rebels for twenty miles in every direction. This is how Reed reported a battle he did not witness: "As the rebels captured [Torreon] quarter by quarter looting began. Panting soldiers fell upon barrels of liquor and broke into stores and private homes. They were to be seen staggering along . . . shouting and singing, while a hellish chatter of rifle fire, the scream of shrapnel and the stab-stab of machine guns steadily killed in the darkness." Perhaps it should be remembered that Stephen Crane also crafted magnificent encounters in the Civil War without ever being at the front.

Nevertheless, with the integrity of a poet, Reed was eminently qualified to relay the following impression of the battle of Torreon: "The exhausted soldiers of both forces fought as in a delirium. Foot by foot Villa's men made their way, house by house, street by street . . . defended by little knots of men until not one was left alive. Panic also seized great numbers who threw down their arms and fled out to the desert in the darkness." Reed was jubilant over the fall of Torreon, telling his readers, "Gen. Villa has won a complete and sweeping victory. The former bandit and refugee is now the absolute master of northern Mexico," adding that the road to Mexico City lay open to him. Actually, as events turned out, Reed overestimated the strength of Villa, not reckoning on the superior tactician Obregon, who was the righthand man of Carranza.

Meanwhile, Reed in El Paso had nothing to pass the time except to chronicle his countrymen's celebration of the fall of Torreon. Saloons, such as "Friend of the Poor" and "Grocery of Good Faith," were jammed to the rafters. Americans, hatless, coatless, and in all manner of attire, rushed to the international bridge in automobiles, on foot, and in street cars to see what was happening.

As Villa racked up more and more victories in northwest and central Mexico, Carranza became fearful that the former bandit would get to Mexico City before his forces under Obregon. This rivalry within the Constitutionalist ranks was duplicated by a schism between journalists covering the scene. Reed remained faithful to Villa, but there was a sharp divergence between Reed and Steffens. The latter attached himself to Carranza, the self-styled

First Chief of the Constitutionalist Army in Charge of the Executive Power, while reportedly denouncing Villa as an "illiterate, unscrupulous, unrevolutionary bandit." Reed took issue with Steffens, his former mentor, writing an article in the *Metropolitan*, "Francisco Villa—The Man of Destiny." Steffens, on the other hand, saw Carranza as the likely victor, and as things turned out, he was right.

On orders from the *World*, Reed went to Nogales on the border to interview the First Chief. The exchange took place in February 1914, but the interview with Carranza did not appear in the *Metropolitan* until September. The delay reflected Reed's hope that the internecine warfare would abate, and the rebels could present a united front. In the interview with "a slightly senile old man, tired and irritated," which took place in a darkened room, he wrote: "As our eyes became accustomed to the light, we saw the gigantic, khaki-clad figure of Don Venustiano Carranza sitting in a big chair, as if he had been placed in it and told not to move. He did not seem to be thinking, nor to have been working . . . You got the impression of a vast, inert body—a statue."

Meanwhile, it is not surprising that Villa was able to recruit from the state of Chihuahua. The disaffected peons were not only poverty stricken, but the Catholic Church and the military buttressed the landed aristocracy. As one man said, "God does not eat. The *curas* [priests] grow fat on us." Most Mexicans were not married because the ritual was so expensive, costing six uninflated pesos, and priests claimed feudal first-night privileges. "The girls here," said one priest, "are very passionate." Because of these and other abuses, Reed wrote, "the Catholic Church in Mexico will never again be the voice of God." Everywhere he went, Reed heard an outcry against the "brutish Catholic Church," or as another Mexican put it, "The priests have exploited us always, under the cloak of religion." He also reported that in the lavish house of Pedro Alvarado, there was a satin seat on the toilet for the priest.

Closely allied with the Church issue was resentment against Spaniards. When Villa entered the city of Chihuahua on November 6, 1914, he declared that all persons of Spanish descent would have to leave the state in five days—later extended to 10 days—or be shot. Reed quoted Villa, "The Spaniards have exploited us for three hundred years. We drove them out twice and allowed them to come back as peaceful citizens."

Next to the Catholic Church, the institution to most feel the brunt of Reed's wrath was the military and the wars in which they engaged. He argued strenuously against United States entry into World War I, which broke out in 1914, drawing on his Mexican experiences to deplore the pain and suffering caused by armed conflict. Reed quoted an ancient Mexican, "Sometimes they attack from Gómez Palacio and sometimes from the mountains. But it is always the same—war. There is something interesting in it for the young, but for us old people, we are tired of war." More personally, he wrote: "I hate soldiers. I hate to see a man with a bayonet fixed on his rifle, who can order me off the street. I hate to belong to an organization that is proud of obeying a caste of superior beings, that is proud of killing free ideas, so that it may the more efficiently kill human beings in cold blood. He concluded, in another article, "No one can have a more utter abhorrence of Militarism than I. No one can wish more heartily that the shame of it may be erased from our century."

It was not all blood and suffering, however, Reed lightened his dispatches with flashes of humor, as the following three examples illustrate. Before the Federal onslaught at La Cadena, "Juan Sánchez stood in front of the *cuartel* [headquarters] sounding reveille; he didn't know which call reveille was, so he played them all." And General Tomás Urbina, noting his camera, shyly asked if he would be good enough to take some pictures for posterity. As Reed recalled the episode:

> For the next hour I took photographs of General Tomás Urbina and his family: General Urbina on foot, with and without sword; General Urbina with and without his family; General Urbina's three children, on horseback and off; General Urbina's mother, and his mistress; the entire family, armed with swords and revolvers; also the phonograph, produced for the purpose; and one of the children holding a placard upon which was inked "General Tomás Urbina R."

When he went to El Paso to file his story on the fall of Torreon, Reed did a piece on the Hotel Cosmopolita. At the gambling tables, he noted "some player, who had lost ten cents, exhausted his vocabulary upon the treasurer, the owner of the place and his ancestors and descendants ten generations each way, and upon God and his family, for allowing such injustice to go unpunished."

When Americans landed Marines at the Gulf city of Veracruz in April 1914, ostensibly after an affront to national honor, Reed was deeply disturbed. Opposed to any kind of intervention in the internal affairs of Mexico, he adamantly lashed out at those who would use the occupation of Veracruz as a springboard to pacify all of Mexico. He was in a tight situation because Villa was the only one of the warring chieftains who did not protest the American incursion at Veracruz, hoping vainly that it would topple Huerta. However, for the first time since the revolution started in 1910, Americans were eager for news about Mexico because their troops were serving on foreign soil. Reed demurred in an editorial, "If We Enter Mexico," published in *Metropolitan* in June 1914, two months after the landing:

> We Americans honestly believe that we will benefit the Mexicans by forcing our institutions upon them. We do not realize that the Latin temperament is differ-

ent from our own—and that their ideal of liberty is broader than ours. We want to debauch the Mexican people and turn into little brown copies of American businessmen and laborers.

There were more than a few troops stationed at the custom-house of Veracruz, however, as the hue and cry intensified for American occupation of Mexico, echoing the sentiment of the nineteenth century for an imperial North America under U.S. auspices. Reed was aghast. Feelings were running white hot, as an unnamed American in Mexico declared to him, "If you write anything to discourage intervention, we'll get you." Nevertheless, Reed told friends he would join Villa's army if the Americans invaded Mexico. And he published an unsigned article in the *New York Times* on April 26, 1914, which quoted Villa: "This quarrel has been between Huerta and the United States, and justly so, but it has not been with the Mexican people." Reed expected Villa to be recognized by the United States after his victory at Torreon, but as it turned out, President Woodrow Wilson extended *de facto* recognition to the Carranza regime in October 1915.

After the interview with the First Chief at Nogales, Reed quoted Carranza:

> I can say positively that intervention would not accomplish what the United States thinks, but would provoke a war which, besides its own consequences, would deepen a profound hatred between both countries, and, moreover, between the United States and the whole of Latin America—a hatred which would endanger the entire future of the United States.

Believing the battle of Torreon would settle the fate of Mexico, Reed thought his work was finished. Therefore, he returned to the United States where he holed up in New York for three months putting together his Mexican dispatches in book form, which was published in 1914 as *Insurgent Mexico*. Before committing his work to permanent form, however, Reed consulted his old Harvard professor, Copeland: "I'm having them send you my *Metropolitan Magazine* war articles on Mexico. If there's anything good in them, it is due entirely to you and English 12. I feel that perhaps they are the first piece of reporting I have done. If they're bad, it's your fault too." Reed dedicated *Insurgent Mexico* to Copeland, an old newspaperman and Boston theater critic with the inscription, "I would never have seen what I did had it not been for your teaching me." Copeland, who was a stern taskmaster, wrote Reed, "You are a born writer—I discovered long ago. But I think you don't work hard enough at writing."

Reed was called back to the traces, however, when Villa, hoping to embroil the United States in the Mexican civil war, killed sixteen American engineers and crossed the border and shot up the town of Columbus, New Mexico on March 9, 1916. In two articles in the *New York American*, Reed's name was prominently displayed in one lead headline and attributed in another byline as a "Noted War Correspondent and Authority on Mexico." From someone who once had dabbled in literature, he had arrived as a reporter, frequently using the techniques of both as later delineated in the New Journalism.

Once again, it was an uphill battle with the American public clamoring for intervention. President Wilson's Mexican policies, constantly shifting, were determined by the information available at the time. Reed was the only expert who had been to Mexico, and he was much in demand. Secretary of State William Jennings Bryan arranged an interview between Reed and Wilson in the White House, but it was fruitless. An expeditionary force under General John J. Pershing entered Mexican territory—with the blessing of Carranza—in search of the elusive Villa. Reed knew this undertaking was hopeless from the start. The "Tiger of the North" knew his plains, deserts, and mountains. The Americans did not.

It is not the purpose of this article to trace Reed beyond Mexico. Suffice it to say that he covered both the western and the eastern fronts in World War I—much to his distaste because he was a pacifist at heart—and he witnessed the Bolshevik revolution in Russia in 1917. He also sat on the executive committee of the Communist International. Lippmann wrote, "[Jack] is the only fellow I know who gets himself pursued by men with revolvers, who is always once more just about to ruin himself." Denied a visa to the United States, he spent time in a Finnish prison and died of typhus in the Soviet Union in 1920 at the age of thirty-three. He was buried at the base of the Kremlin Wall along with three other Americans, the highest honor the former Soviet Union could bestow on a foreigner. On the other hand, Russian censors edited and later banned *Ten Days That Shook the World*, his masterwork of the Russian revolution. Later translated into many languages, the book mentioned Joseph Stalin only twice.

Some might say New Journalism faded from the scene with the passing of the 1960s and 1970s, but it left a legacy of a new way of looking at news in the age of electronic communications. The original furor over this frontal assault on formula writing or the inverted pyramid, dating back to the Civil War, really pertained to book-length reportage, such as Truman Capote's *In Cold Blood*. Using fictional techniques, a greater truth was thought to emerge, but not everyone agreed. They denounced the new genre as "journalit" or "parajournalism" and claimed it actually dated back to the novelists of the early nineteenth century. But Norman Mailer's nonfiction also was regarded as a journalistic breakthrough since it was "charged with the energy of art," according to J.E. Murphy in 1974.

The question arises as to how far the "New Journalism," or its successor, "Literary Journalism," can go without twisting the facts. Reed did not invent incidents in the same sense as Janet Cooke, a reporter for the *Washington Post* who wrote a spurious story of an eight-year-old heroin addict. He did report the fall of Torreon five days before it happened, based on reports of those fleeing the beleaguered city and Reed's intimate knowledge of Villa's tactics. *But* he spoke with authority.

Scholars agree. Gregory Mason wrote in *Outlook* on May 6, 1925, "It is true that Reed loved a good story too much to spoil one by over-fidelity to scientific exactitude." Jim Tuck added that *Insurgent Mexico* is "a hybrid, a work that is part fact and part fabrication. Reed did not so much invent as embroider." The good and the bad were incorporated in an anonymous review in the *Outlook* on October 21, 1914: "Mr. Reed does not argue or preach; he simply pictures Mexico in revolution; his picture is by no means complete; one feels at times that it is a rapid fire of snap-shots, but it bears the marks of truthful delineation, and it is remarkably vivid."

Perhaps the work habits of Reed are best illustrated by an incident in which a belligerent soldier accosted Reed in his hotel room, and the journalist by his adroit salesmanship traded his watch for his life. This encounter merited only six words in Reed's notes, "Watch given to Capt. Antonio García," yet this scrap of human interest became two pages of *Insurgent Mexico*. In this case, as throughout Reed's work, the reader was the beneficiary, privy to the inner drama of events.

Another aspect of Reed's career that was questionable was his latching onto Villa as the savior of Mexico. This was not something new for journalists to do in Latin America or in world history. For Reed, the man of the hour was Villa, while Steffens saw greater promise in Carranza, which turned out to be a wise choice. Both journalists treated their man as their "baby" who really could do no wrong. The ascendancy of this chosen one on the battlefield or in the administration of internal affairs was thus intimately tied up with each reporter's own journalistic ambitions. Whether Edgar Snow with Mao Tsetung or Herbert Matthews with Fidel Castro, the affinity for good copy sometimes clouded good judgment.

During his lifetime, Reed was a character in a play and two novels, and after his death, despite the Cold War, he was the subject of seven biographies. When *Insurgent Mexico* came out in 1914, it met with mixed reactions. Dos Passos was laudatory, writing in the *Harvard Monthly* in November 1914 that Reed, "neither dogmatizes nor puts forward any panacea for the ills of Mexico. . . .The book as a whole contains some of the finest impressionistic descriptions of the life and scenery of Mexico that have ever appeared."

In a moment of despondency, Reed questioned all he had fought for throughout his life on three continents. In his autobiographical fragment, written four years before his death, he said, "But I am not sure anymore that the working class is capable of revolution, peaceful or otherwise; the workers are so divided and bitterly hostile to each other, so badly led, so blind to their class interest." His disillusionment stemmed in part from that part of his character that was essentially romantic, in the view of two of his biographers. Both seem to use the term "romantic" rather than "impractical" or "visionary" or "idealistic" even though the latter two terms seem to fit Reed best. A committed writer, he was less interested in Marxist dialectics than the reality around him. After his death in 1920, he was claimed by both Communists and non-Communists as their own.

He once said that the two most important persons in his life were Steffens, although they split on the Mexican Revolution, and Copeland, his teacher of composition at Harvard. These are excerpts of a eulogy written by Steffens in *The Freeman* on November 3, 1920:

> John Reed, American poet, died, a communist, in Moscow, the capitol of the future State, of the disease of the revolutionary present: typhus; he was bitten by a sick louse, a doomed parasite. . . .You see, in Moscow, in Soviet Russia, where there are lice and hunger and discipline and death; where it is hell now; they see—even a non-Communist can see something to live or to die for.

But perhaps the most moving tribute came from Lippmann, his Harvard classmate who went on to become the dean of American letters. While Reed was still alive, Lippmann wrote in the *New Republic* on December 26, 1914:

> I don't know what to do about him [Reed]. In common with a whole regiment of his friends, I have been brooding over his soul for years, and often I feel like saying to him what one of them said when Reed was explaining Utopia, "If I were establishing it, I'd hang you first, my dear Jack." But it would be a lonely Utopia."

(Jerry W. Knudson, "John Reed, A Reporter in Revolutionary Mexico," *Journalism History*, 29:2, Summer 2003. Reprinted by permission of *Journalism History*).

IN QUEST OF EMILIANO ZAPATA
BY JERRY W. KNUDSON

When I approached the tourist center in 1961 in downtown Mexico City during a break from graduate study at the University of Virginia, I was on a pilgrimage seeking the reality of the historic Emiliano Zapata, the southern guerrilla fighter and agrarian reform leader in the Mexican Revolution which began in 1910. At the tourist center, I enquired about bus schedules to the town of Cuautla, in the heart of Zapata country off the central plateau and only about thirty miles away. "Oh, you don't want to go there," a young woman at the center told me. "Nothing ever happens there."

Nothing ever happens in Cuautla, cradle of the agrarian revolt which in 1909 touched off the first great social and economic revolution of the 20th century? It began seven years before the Bolshevik upheaval in Russia, but Americans know little about what happened at their very doorstep. The military phase of the Mexican Revolution lasted more than seven years. Although this long struggle cost some one million Mexican lives, reforms were not codified until the Constitution of 1917, including Article 23 which spelled out land reform in a country dominated by large landowners and the Mexican Catholic Church.

As my bus threaded its way down the escarpment from the central plateau to the sub-tropical state of Morelos with its sugar-cane fields and where Cuautla is located, I could imagine the white-clad men of Morelos half a century earlier attacking Federal soldiers who had been abusing them under the 35-year dictatorship of Porfirio Diaz, then melting away into their corn fields to regroup and strike again. It was guerrilla warfare with almost beautiful precision. As one writer put it, when Tepoztlan was occupied by the Federales, townspeople came down at night from their mountain hideaways behind the town to rob their own fruit trees.

When the bus arrived at Cuautla, I found a cheerful and overweight taxi driver—the only one in town—and asked if he could take me to some of the survivors who had fought with Zapata. "Sure," he said with pride, "Hop in!" It turned out that the town boasted two *zapatistas*—living remnants of the peasant rebellion—one man and one woman both in their late eighties and revered by all.

First on our itinerary was Ricarda Ayonn, who came out to greet me in a faded house dress and curious eyes. She was a heavy-set woman with sagging breasts but great dignity. It should be noted that women also fought in the Revolution or supported their men by cooking and binding up wounds, sometimes on the tops of careening boxcars. In the arid north railroads were essential to transport men and supplies for long distances.

Ricarda looked me over before I asked the inevitable question, "Why did you fight?" Being a graduate student in history, I expected some profound social and economic reason that would knock the socks off my professor. Why did she fight? Ricarda looked at me and laughed, with a twinkle in her eye, "All of the young men of the village had gone to fight. There was nothing doing around here!"

As for Policarpo Castro, the other *zapatista* survivor in town, he got up from his sick bed in his dingy little hut and came out to see what was going on. He was old and frail but not defeated. He spoke with his head bowed and speculating eyes. Why did he fight? Without hesitation, he replied, "Land! They took all our land!" And with great pride he showed me a little corner of the land he had fought for. I thanked him for his courtesy and kindness, and as I walked away he called after me in a vibrant voice despite his age, the slogan of Zapata's rebellion, *Tierra y Libertad!* (Land and Liberty).

Zapata, guerrilla leader of the campesinos whose land had been stripped away by chicanery or force through the centuries, had fought every regime in Mexico City, after fighting broke out in 1909, *since* agrarian reform was not delivered. The mal-distribution of land in the hands of overbearing *patrones* or bosses was a national problem.

More statues of Emiliano Zapata appear in the countryside and cities than those of any other national hero. In the little village of Anenecuilco where Ricarda and Policarpo were living out their lives, Emiliano Zapata became one of them, and they of him. The Mexican government today has erected a modern, circular white-stone monument around the remains of the adobe hut where Emiliano was born. But practically nobody goes to the place where he died, the remote hacienda of San Juan de Chinameca, not reachable by road. My taxi driver, huffing and puffing, and a little boy who somehow joined our entourage, walked the final two or three miles through corn fields to reach the hacienda building where Zapata was assassinated in 1919. The boy, who undoubtedly had never seen an American before, skipped backwards ahead of us, hitching up his pants from time to time, in order ot get a good look at me, the gringo. Children were playing soccer in the foreground as we reached the hacienda building itself, a fortress-like building which dominated and protected the patron's holdings, perhaps one or two blocks long and three or four stories high.

Here, on a cool crisp April morning in 1919, Emiliano Zapata and a few men rode up to parley with Major Jesus Guajardo, a Federal officer who had pretended to defect from the forces of the ruling Venustiano Carranza in order to entrap Zapata. Guajardo offered arms and ammunition to arrange the meeting. Outside the hacienda courtyard, as Zapata and his men dismounted and entered the arched gateway, files of Federal soldiers raised their rifles, ostensibly to salute the distinguished visitor, but instead they brought the weapons to their shoulders and blasted away at point blank. The marks of that deadly fusillade are still there, deep scars not only on the arched gateway but in the minds of many Mexican people.

At the time of Zapata's assassination, it seemed that the hopes of Morelos and other states in central Mexico fell with him. The Federales dumped his body in the center of the plaza of Cuautla for all to see, to convince them that their savior was no more. But the campesinos refused to believe it. Looking at the corpse, one said, "That is not 'Miliano.' He had a mole on his left cheek." Others found discrepancies elsewhere on the body before them. They would not let Emiliano die.

John Womack, Jr. who has written the definitive biography of Zapata (1968) has put it best, "The belief that he [Zapata] had not died was a consolation, both for shame at not fighting any more and for anguish at having charged him with an impossible responsibility, having trusted him to death."

Two years later I went back to Cuautla for the commemoration every year of the death of Emiliano Zapata. I expected to see a handful of old men weaving from one cantina to another, but instead the entire plaza was surrounded with huge floral wreaths from ejidos (village communal lands which Zapata had tried to protect). It was more than a half a century later, but one would have thought the man died yesterday. Old men murmured to themselves as they read the inscriptions on the wreaths to make sure no one had forgotten. A bureaucrat from Mexico City stood on the speaker's platform making a flowery speech, but his back was turned to the massed campesinos. He was talking only to the other bureaucrats on the platform, but the men below weren't listening, anyway. They had heard it all before. They had come to pay their respects to Emiliano.

When the *Wall Street Journal* in 1994 tried to rewrite the Zapata legacy as an antidote to the rebellion in the southernmost state of Chiapas, few of us could keep a straight face. They quoted Mateo Zapata, who at 77 was the youngest of the three surviving children, as opposing use of the Zapata name by the EZLN (Frente Zapatista de Liberacion Nacional), by the rebelling group in Chiapas. (The United States press completely ignored the spark which set off the rebellion—namely the "modernization of agriculture" proposed by NAFTA (North American Free Trade Association) which in Chiapas would have meant the destruction of the ancient *ejidos* which the original Zapata and his followers had fought so hard to save. Not a single newspaper or commentator in the United States noted that the Chiapas rebellion, which initially cost more than 100 lives, broke out on January 1, 1993, the very day that NAFTA took effect. The connection was obvious.

I remember well when I met Mateo Zapata in 1961, the youngest of Zapata's five children who now is in his late seventies and holds a minor civil service job in Cuautla. He said he would meet me in the plaza, and I was shocked when he came around the corner of the building where I was standing. He was the spitting image of his father at that age, according to photographs. One could sense that this soft-spoken man did not want any intrusion on his father's memory. I asked if I could photograph him beside the statue of his father in the center of the plaza, a statue of Zapata on horseback, with a protective arm around the shoulders of a campesino standing by. Mateo Zapata politely declined to be photographed there, and I felt like a foolish tourist. But he did let me photograph him against the side of the building, and there he is on my office wall, with his level gaze and honest face. Of the other two surviving children, Anita runs a cafe in Cuautla and Nicolas, it is said, has become a large landholder in the region.

The *Wall Street Journal* writer, Paul B. Carroll, claimed one of Emiliano's slogans was "Land, Water, Justice and Law." That's news to me, as I had never come across such a slogan in the Mexican Revolution. More disturbing, Carroll goes on to say, "He [Mateo Zapata] has also put together something called the Plan de Ayala, which hopes to restore land to peasants." Obviously, Carroll did not do his homework before charging off to Mexico. The Plan of Ayala was formulated by Mateo's father early in the Revolution. [In Latin American culture, every uprising must be justified by a plan or *pronunciamento* setting forth the goals of the revolt]. The Plan of Ayala was drafted in the mountain hideaway of Zapata, with the advice of his old school teacher Emilio Montano. [It is not true that Zapata could not read or write. He had the equivalent of a third-grade education, however rudimentary, and in the *legajos*—large bundles of documents wrapped in brown paper and bound with twine—from the state of Morelos, now in the National Archives but uncatalogued, one may find Zapata's signature and his notations in the margins of papers or orders of the day.

Actually, the Plan of Ayala was visionary. But not to those few men who stepped forward to sign it on that mountain top. It called for the great landowners to give up one-third of their vast holdings—to be distributed among the landless peasants. If the landowners refused to do this, all of their lands would be confiscated, and of the remaining two-thirds, one third would go to continue prosecuting the war, and the final third to the widows and orphans of the fallen soldiers. A sympathetic priest with a typewriter was hustled from a nearby village to type three copies of the Plan of Ayala.

One smudged copy of this historic document made its way to Mexico City and the offices of the only capital newspaper, *Diario del Hogar* (Home Daily) which had supported the *zapatista* cause. All of the other newspapers, staunch conservatives, either ignored Zapata or attacked him viciously. This undermined the fragile democratic government of Francisco I. Madero, making him seem weak and vulnerable. This led to the counter-revolution by General Victoriano Huerta, whom diplomats had to search the bars of Mexico City to find him to transact business. It also led to the murder of Madero and his Vice-President Pino Suarez and plunged Mexico into four more years of bloodshed.

On balance, the Plan of Ayala has been ignored by some historians as completely unrealistic and therefore of little importance, but it was symbolic of the aspirations of masses of Mexican peons. They had something to continue fighting for. The intellectual author of the Plan has been disputed. Was it his old schoolteacher, the anarchist Otilio Montano, whom Zapata later purged?

Actually, according to my interview in a small, cheap apartment near Chapultepec Hill in Mexico City, it was Antonio Diaz Soto y Gama, a young Marxist lawyer in 1910 who sought to win over Zapata to his ideology at the latter's mountain retreat. Soto y Gama in my interview said he spent a whole afternoon trying to persuade Zapata to come out for communism. Zapata was nothing if not polite. He listened carefully through the long, hot afternoon to what his guest had to say, and then finally Zapata himself spoke up. "That's all very interesting," he said, "but by any chance was this Carlos Marx a farmer?"

Did Zapata really say that? Oral history can be valuable in reconstructing recent events, but there are caveats all over the place. The old man sitting at the linoleum-covered kitchen table with me talked with earnestness and conviction. Yet memories fade or are embellished with time. I had my doubts until Antonio Diaz Soto y Gama rummaged around in a dresser drawer and gave me a faded typewritten copy of the Plan of Ayala. It was not one of the original three copies, but rather another copy which a friend had made for him at the time. When this old man, reduced almost to squalor, looked me in the eye and gave me his only copy of the Plan of Ayala so it would live on, I knew he was telling the truth.

Chapter Two

Bolivia: Revolution in the Clouds

The capital of La Paz seems scooped out of a lunar landscape, unfolding downward in a broad canyon from the high level plain of the *altiplano*, which is the site of El Alto airport. Its runways were lengthened with United States aid to accommodate jet planes in the rarified atmosphere. (The United States was also responsible for the first highway connecting La Paz and Santa Cruz, second largest city in Bolivia, opening up the rich agricultural possibilities of the East). In 1952, the same year that the Bolivian revolution broke out, President-elect Dwight D. Eisenhower sent his brother Milton Eisenhower, then president of Kansas State University, on a fact-finding trip around Latin America. Upon his return, he convinced his brother that the United States should support the Bolivian National Revolution with all means at our disposal because it was democratic, and the aid was desperately needed.

As scholar James W. Wilkie has pointed out, at the time we did support Bolivia with more aid per capita than any other country in the world. Without this assistance, Bolivia might have slipped back into its old feudal pattern of military men hungry for power.

At the airport, when we taxied to the gate, I looked out the window and noticed a sign which proudly proclaimed that La Paz was 13,404 feet above sea level, the highest capital in the world (Lhasa, Tibet, by comparison, is a mere 11,830 feet). By a quirk of history, however, the Supreme Court and National Library and Archives are in Sucre, the original capital, 435 miles from La Paz.

At El Alto airport it takes time to accustom oneself to the thin air of Bolivia. Following the advice of my Latin American history professor, I was the last to leave the plane, allowing a few moments of climate adjustment, although I still had to sit on my suitcase going through customs, somewhat weak and breathless.

It takes about a week to get over the severe form of *siroche* or "mountain sickness." The folk remedy for those from the lowlands is to stretch out on a park bench, face covered with a newspaper, and well fortified with *pisco*, the national drink. Curiously enough, on numerous later trips I had no difficulty at all with the altitude.

At the time, the distinguished British historian Arnold J. Toynbee, touring Latin America, wanted to come to La Paz from Lima, Peru to witness a social revolution in its very early stages, but his doctors dissuaded him because of the effect the altitude might have on his heart condition.

The French, who take revolutions seriously, were early on the scene, with a little book by Noël Pierre Lenoir, translated into *Revolución Altitud 4,000 Metros* (1958). But the first to inform the United States audience about what was happening in the high Andes was Robert J. Alexander of Rutgers University whose book, *The Bolivian National Revolution* (also 1958), set the parameters for others, until the revisionists took over.

When Evo Morales, 46, an Aymará Indian, was elected President of Bolivia in 2005, he became the first indigenous head of state there since the time of the Incas some 300 years ago. It was both a symbolic and real advance for both the dominant Quechua and minority Aymará peoples, who together comprise about 60 percent of the population of Bolivia, but had been denied any participation in national life for centuries. *The Movimiento Nacionalista Revolucionario* (Nationalist Revolutionary Movement, MNR, 1952–1964 and beyond), Latin America's second social and economic revolution, after that which began in Mexico in 1910, extended the vote to all Bolivians in 1952, which planted the seeds for the triumph of Morales half a century later.

Before, suffrage had been restricted to literate, property-owning males 30 or older, about only 10 percent of the population—the elite of whites (of Spanish descent) or upper-class *cholos* (of mixed race) which excluded entirely from national life both Quechua and Aymará "campesinos" (literally, "men of the fields," a designation used more widely when the word *indio* or "Indian" was officially banned after the MNR Revolution began after 1952 as a reminder of past servitude.

As anthropologist Paul Radin has noted, "Of few mature and complex civilizations has time, corruption and exploitation taken so devastating a toll as that of the Aymará and Quechua." (*Indians of South America*, p. 277). A Bolivian put it even more strongly. Gustavo A. Navarro (pen-name Tristán Marof) wrote as early as 1934, "No people have been so subjected, in such absolute form, as the Indian people [of Bolivia]. The very Jews under the rule of the Pharaohs still had their leaders, their religion and their prophets. But the [Bolivian] Indian has been stripped of everything, from his land to his way of thinking." (*La trageda del altiplano*, p. 42).

In Bolivia, campesinos, mostly illiterate and exploited for centuries, whether during the colonial or national periods, spoke only their own languages and not Spanish, the only language heard in the halls of power. For the Indians, the only recourse was to withdraw into a deep psychological and physical isolation. Today, after the MNR reforms, debates in the national Congress are conducted in both Spanish and Quechua. The latter is the major language of Bolivia.

Thus, it was a long struggle for political awareness to develop among these peoples, although in recent years massive demonstrations, mainly over Bolivian control of her natural gas reserves, largest in Latin America and now the country's main source of revenue, deposed two elite interim presidents. "We vote with our feet," one campesino told me.

When Evo Morales, of humble origin, was inaugurated, he stood on the balcony of the Congress building in La Paz addressing a mass of Aymará and Quechua peoples in the Plaza Murillo below. He was flanked by the heads of state of eleven nations who had come to honor him. He and his populist political party, Movement Toward Socialism, which had won the election of 2005 by 51 percent of the vote, may have been only a beginning, but for them it must have been a glorious beginning.

Their voices—along with those of other Bolivians who sympathized with their cause—at last were being heard. The world press was captivated by an Indian president of Bolivia. The first act of President Morales was to perform the ancient rites of his ancestors in full ceremonial dress at the ruins of Tiahuanaco, cradle of Aymará culture and believed by some archaeologists to have been the first planned city complex in the Americas. The historian Hubert Herring once wrote that the history of the first Americans must be written in soft chalk, easily erased and corrected, as new discoveries come to light.

A few years ago, cave paintings discovered near Oruro in central Bolivia revealed that humans had penetrated that far south from their Asian homeland and the bridge of North America by 15,000 B.C., much earlier than previously thought. A woman correspondent for the BBC and I were so fascinated visiting that cave that we missed our two-car train at nearby Oruro for a meeting in Potosí. Typically Bolivian, the station master radioed ahead, and the train actually stopped and waited for us until we caught up with them after a wild taxi ride on a road, if you could call it that, with dust inches deep. When we got there, the waiting passengers did not complain.

The *New York Times* missed the significance of the election of Evo Morales, however, repeatedly referring to "the leftward drift" of Latin America, since both Fidel Castro of Cuba and Hugo Chávez of Venezuela had supported the electoral campaign of Morales, forging what some humorous partisan dubbed "an Axis of Good." The *Times* found it all very quaint and rustic, depicting Morales as "a former llama herder" (November 3, 2005) and "a former coca farmer" (November 19, 2005) and one lead sentence which described him as "The son of a shepherd who grew up in an adobe home in the frigid highlands" (January 23, 2006).

Those responsible for these articles seemed not to realize that here was the opening chapter every bit as important as the beginning of the end of apartheid in South Africa and Rhodesia, with Indians replacing blacks in what I once described as "the majority as minority."

Evo Morales had his moment on the world stage, however. He began a ten-day whirlwind tour in which he was warmly received by President Jacques Chirac of France, Ho Jintao of the People's Republic of China, Prime Minister José Luís Rodríguez of Spain and others.

Morales was not invited to the United States, although a special envoy was later sent to congratulate him, perhaps because of friction between the two countries over U.S. efforts to substitute other cash crops in Bolivia for coca, the plant from which cocaine is derived, since Bolivia is the third largest grower in Latin America, after Colombia and Peru.

Morales in fact got his political start unionizing coca growers around the Lake Chapare region. The defense offered by these coca producers, which I have heard many times, is simply, "If you [the United States] wouldn't buy it, we wouldn't grow it." Moreover, chewing coca leaves by campesinos is a way of life in Bolivia, producing a mild narcotic effect that relieves both hunger and distress. When he appeared before the United Nations, a smiling Morales impishly held up a coca leaf, a much more effective gesture than the "devil" harangue of Hugo Chávez of Venezuela.

In twelve short years (1952–1964) Bolivia nationalized the major tin mines to establish its power base among the 35,000 miners (although the tin veins are now being depleted, and some mines have again been privatized). But in 1952 this action had enormous symbolic effect and promoted labor reforms in the mines. (Some foreign technicians maliciously destroyed their equipment before leaving Bolivia.)

Natural gas, Bolivia's hope for the future since tin is no longer king, now belongs to Bolivia. Quechua and Aymará workers take a quite different view of the country's natural resources than their European or American counterparts. The land and its bounty are to be respected. As one miner said to me in Spanish but with native eloquence, "They [the foreign mining companies] leave us only holes in our mountains and holes in the lungs of our miners."

The Big Three Bolivian tin magnates were even worse. Simón I. Patiño was reputed to be the sixth wealthiest man in the world, living in luxury in Europe while his miners lived in squalor in Bolivia. Augusto Céspedes, MNR militant and outstanding Bolivian writer, told me that his thinly disguised novel of Patiño's indifference and cruelty to his workers *Metal del Diablo* (The Devil's Metal) was scheduled to be made into a movie. The producers even brought Céspedes to Hollywood as technical adviser for the film, but before production could begin, the Patiño family suppressed the project, according to Céspedes. He loved being photographed with movie stars.

Bolivia has always been a mono-cultural economy, dependent on silver in the colonial period, tin in the national period, and now natural gas. Thus, the Bolivian National Revolution, however spasmodic, underwent a military interregnum (1964–1982) but even though the military largely did not advance the MNR reforms, neither did they dismantle them.

The Bolivian National Revolution, as noted, by granting the universal vote in 1952, was more democratic than the transformation of Cuba under Fidel Castro after 1959. In the early years at least, Castro could have won any honest election hands down, but he chose to fashion his own style of government, best analyzed in Theodore Draper's *Castroism, Theory and Practice* (first published in the United Kingdom in 1965 and in the United States in 1969).

As for Bolivia, some, including the 23-year-old Ernesto "Che" Guevara, writing in *The Motorcycle Diaries, Notes on a Latin American Journey* (published in 2003), that what he personally observed in Bolivia in the early 1950s was "reformist" and not revolutionary. (Che also was not satisfied with the Guatemalan reforms of Jacobo Arbenz (1950–1954), which brought down the wrath of the CIA). But to me, the gradual emergence of the Aymará and Quechua peoples into national life in Bolivia through the universal vote after centuries of denial of their very existence by the white or mixed power structure, is truly revolutionary, although it has been and will continue to be a slow process in bringing fully into that national life.

As late as 1971, for example, there were only 23 campesinos (and five women) among the 218 delegates to the ten-day Popular Assembly, billed as the first labor governing body since the Soviet of 1917 or the Paris Commune of 1878. The low interest in Latin American events was evidenced when only two foreign observers showed up for the Popular Assembly—a correspondent for the official Soviet news agency TASS, who disappeared after the first day, which was only ceremonial, and me (not having press credentials at the time, I flashed my University of Kentucky library card, which satisfied the guards, who then frisked me and let me in). But in the crowd somehow I wound up in the *fabriles* (textile workers) section until someone politely led me to the small press box above the Assembly floor.

For ten days, the campesinos and miners packing the balconies vented their anger, with uproars at times deafening and lasting as long as half an hour before Juan Lechín, the durable labor leader, could get the "co-legislators" in the balconies to come to order.

Before the Popular Assembly could reconvene a few weeks later, however, populist General Juan José Torres, who had sanctioned it, was overthrown in the most violent encounter in La Paz since the 1952 revolt. I was about to go out and get my dry cleaning when I heard the crack of gunfire in the center of La Paz. It was a long night of street fighting and mortars lobbed randomly throughout the city to terrorize the people. Church bells rang incessantly in a futile attempt to restore order to the city.

Later, newspaper photos showed resisters, along with Juan Lechín, looking like a figure in a Greek tragedy, building street barricades with cobblestones from the street themselves. The next day, I witnessed the aerial bombardment of the University of San Andrés, Bolivia's institution of highest learning, and the hold-out students later being herded down the street by members of the *Falange Socialista Boliviana* (modeled on the Falange of Franco's Spain) in business suits and dark glasses, kicking and beating the students.

The overthrow of Torres, later assassinated in Argentina, was a severe blow to Bolivian labor, and was the occasion of the most bizarre political union in Bolivian history—that of the leftwing MNR and rightwing Falange. Talking to a shopkeeper a few days later, I exclaimed, "I don't believe it!" And he shrugged and replied, "In Bolivia, Señor, all things are possible!" During the scramble for power after the fall of Torres, one image I would rather not remember was that of Paz Estenssoro jumping on top of a car in downtown La Paz and shouting, "I am the *caudillo* [strongman] of Bolivia!" I thought at the time that this pathetic display marked the end of the career of one of the great democrats of the Americas. But he surfaced again later and refound the presidency he so cherished (1985–1989) which helped pull Bolivia out of hyper-inflation. He also found time, through the United States ambassador, to commend me for my book, *Bolivia: Press and Revolution, 1932–1964* (1986).

As events unfolded, to most observers this indeed was a social revolution. The MNR, which did not call itself a political party, thereby hoping to embrace various political persuasions in Bolivian society, was partly a backlash to Bolivia's humiliating defeat to Paraguay in the disastrous Chaco War (1932–1935) which began over a senseless boundary dispute, poorly demarcated since the Spanish considered Bolivia as Upper Peru, and ultimately claimed the lives of 52,000 Bolivians and 36,000 Paraguayans. This was the greatest carnage in the western hemisphere since our own Civil War, although at the time, the world took little notice, and the League of Nations was powerless to act in its first test before the Italian invasion of Abyssinia (Ethiopia).

In 1932, when war was formally declared, readers in La Paz had no more idea of what the extensive and isolated Chaco in southern Bolivia was like than the far side of the moon. Of the three major dailies of La Paz, owned or controlled by the Big Three mine owners, also called the "tin barons," *El Diario* (Simón I. Patiño), *Ultima Hora* (Mauricio Hochschild) and *La Razón* (Carlos Víctor Aramayo), only the latter even bothered to send a correspondent to the Chaco front, and only Hochschild deigned to live in Bolivia.

Bolivian dissidents, called "the Generation of the Chaco," were appalled by the incompetence of the military commanders, who it was said showed up only for the cocktail hour at the mud and wattle forts (no trees in the Chaco and little water), connected by trenches. A generation of Bolivian writers also attacked the indifference of the public, and thus aroused the national social conscience through literature and the press.

WELLSPRINGS OF REVOLT

Bolivia, on the other hand, produced three men whose books and newspaper work helped to instigate and carry through a social revolution. Foremost among these writers was Carlos Montenegro, whose *Nacionalismo y coloniaje* (Nationalism and Colonialism) of 1943 was an affirmative call to greater national self-awareness. Before Montenegro, Bolivian letters had been dominated by the pessimism and defeatism of Alcides Argüedas' classic *Pueblo enfermo* (Sick People) of 1909, with its notorious dictum, "Wherever you push your finger in Bolivian life, you will produce pus." Disdain and deprecation were considered stylish after Argüedas. As late as the Chaco War, for example, a Bolivian president was quoted as saying, "You can plant turnips on the shoulders of the Bolivian people." Montenegro felt the attitude spawned by Argüedas was pathological, with Bolivia doomed to morbid introspection unless the underlying causes of its semi-colonial economic subordination were revealed and righted.

Montenegro found Bolivian literature slavishly imitative of Argüedas, casting up only the reprehensible in national life. But Montenegro also scored the oligarchical press which he felt held the country in the throes of a chronic inferiority complex. It was no secret to anyone that the Big Three tin magnates held sway in the La Pax daily press. Simón I. Patiño held a controlling interest in *El Diario*, the dean of the capital's press, having been founded by Manual Carrasco in 1904. Mauricio Hochschild dominated *Ultima Hora*, which was frequently called "the tin elephant of the afternoon" by its MNR opponent, *La Calle*. Carlos Víctor Aramayo owned *La Razón* outright. *La Razón* was to be the first victim of the Bolivian National Revolution. It never published again after the 1952 revolt, although many Bolivians believed that its death was a case of suicide rather than murder.

These newspapers, in Montenegro's view, were servile to interests alien to Bolivian nationhood. Hochschild, a German Jew naturalized in Argentina, was the only one of the Big Three who resided in Bolivia. Antenor Patiño, son of the discoverer of tin at Llallagua at the close of the Nineteenth Century, was reputed to be the world's fifth richest man, yet he seldom visited the sources of his wealth. Thus Montenegro argued that the three La Paz daily newspapers supported the kind of elite government that would allow the Big Three to continue to take out of Bolivia tin earnings which made up 76 percent of the country's production. Moreover, Montenegro argued, the daily journalism of La Paz, depending as it did on western wire services, was alien to the Indian and *cholo* (mixed) culture of Bolivia. Montenegro continued:

"But the greatest wound which capitalist journalism inflicted on our people was creating a cunning and artificial way of thinking in the Bolivian literate classes. . . . The public did not have, throughout half a century, any other source of cultural nutrition than journalism, and it learned to attend to and to judge things in consultation with the printed [newspaper] page. This was little less than an oracle for current opinion."

The MNR always held Montenegro foremost among its intellectual precursors. As *La Nación* noted in 1955, "The debt which our people owes him is that he gave back the panoramic vision of our history, demonstrating that a scientific comprehension of our past and our present was possible, in order to establish the bases for a future." Before Montenegro, the newspaper continued, Bolivia had always been at the margin of history, consisting of "a small self-contained world of castes and feudal struggles." But Montenegro's scalpel cut through Bolivian life to expose a sharp national duality, and he urged the solidarity of men of the cities with the exploited of the mines and countryside.

Born in Cochabamba in 1903, Montenegro was extremely active in journalism before his premature death from cancer in 1953 in New York. He was the director of the *Semanario Busch*, a weekly published in La Paz in 1941 as the official organ of the nascent MNR. The paper was named for Colonel Germán Busch, reform military ruler of Bolivia from 1937 until his suicide in 1939. The MNR claimed Busch as a martyr, owing to the pressures exerted upon him by *la rosca*, the Bolivian elite which had instigated the Chaco War and profited from it. Montenegro also contributed extensively to *La Calle*, which lasted from its founding in 1936 until it was closed down by the military government of General Enrique Peñaranda in 1943. For these journalistic activities, Montenegro was imprisoned along with others in the tropical province of Velasco in 1941, accused of having helped plan an alleged *putsch* against the oligarchical government of Peñaranda. Montenegro was also under suspicion for having served as secretary general of the new

Partido Socialista (Socialist Party) in 1936. But he continued to write under the pseudonym of "Kisiabó" from a prison camp in the interior.

Once a secondary school teacher and lawyer who defended the poor, Montenegro was named Minister of Agriculture in the cabinet of Major Gualberto Villarroel (1943–1946), who headed Bolivia's first abortive reform movement, and in 1944 he became ambassador to Mexico. During the *sexenio*, the six-year period from the overthrow of Villarroel in 1946 to the successful MNR revolution of 1952, Montenegro founded and directed the review "SEA" or *Síntesis Económica Americana* (American Economic Synthesis) in Buenos Aires where he supported himself by working on the prestigious Argentine newspaper, *La Prensa*. Dissatisfied with what he regarded as the biased and frequently erroneous reports of the wire services, Montenegro founded the short-lived *Intercontinental de Periodistas* (Journalists' Intercontinental Service), an independent group of writers from the underdeveloped Latin American countries. After the 1952 revolution he was named Bolivia's ambassador to neighboring Chile.

Yet Montenegro's crowning service to the Bolivian revolutionary cause was his book, *Nacionalismo y coloniaje*, which justified Bolivia's seizure of Standard Oil holdings in 1937 and urged nationalization of the Big Three tin mines. As *La Nación* later pointed out, Montenegro's book outlined the philosophy for the militancy of the MNR. "It demonstrates that the theoretical conception which the party sustains should be as monolithic as the form of its organization." (The MNR was organized in a hierarchy of 45 departmental or provincial commands throughout the country to insure discipline.) Another writer stated in *La Nación* that Montenegro "formed the revolutionary generation that fights today for our country."

AUGUSTO CÉSPEDES, SOCIAL REALIST

Augusto Céspedes was both soldier in the Chaco and later correspondent there for *El Universal*, the only Bolivian newspaper which opposed the war. His *Sangre de Mestizos* (Blood of Half-Breeds) depicted the plight of campesinos and *cholos* who were hauled to the faraway front in the uninhabited Chaco, speaking only their own languages and ordered to fight for an incomprehensible cause, many not even knowing what the word "Bolivia" meant. Rumors of oil in the Chaco complicated matters as the conflict became an international (although surrogate) issue, with the United States (Standard Oil) supporting Bolivia and Great Britain and Argentina backing Paraguay (Royal Dutch Shell). Modern weaponry flowed to both sides.

Sangre de Mestizos, acidic vignettes of the reality of the Chaco War, based on thirty-four dispatches by Céspedes to *El Universal*, which I collected and later were published in La Paz in book form, *Crónicas heróicas de una guerra estúpida* (Heroic Stories of a Stupid War, 1975). Little known in the United States, Céspedes was one of only three Latin American writers invited to a literary congress in the Soviet Union in 1971, although he abhorred Marxism-Leninism. But his literary depiction of men at war equals that of such writers as John Reed during the Mexican Revolution or Ernie Pyle in World War II.

At the time, there were only eleven newspapers in all of Bolivia, including only one outside of La Paz national, *Los Tiempos* of Cochabamba. To combat this solid monopoly of the press (except for *El Universal*) which in effect shaped the destiny of Bolivia, appealing to the ten percent of the elite who could vote, Armando Arce founded an audacious newspaper for the MNR, *La Calle* (The Street, 1933–1946). Its very name indicated that it was willing to take to the streets to wage war against entrenched privilege. It captivated Bolivia's thin middle class, supportive of reform. Above all else, *La Calle* made its points with ironic humor, such as this item from the famous column, *Callejón Oscuro* (Dark Alley), "The government has created a burial allotment for school teachers and their families so that these can now die of hunger with complete confidence." (March 17, 1936)

Thus, winning over the middle sector, if it can be called that, enabled the MNR finally to gain power with only some 600 casualties in street fighting in La Paz and Oruro on April 9–11, 1952. In power, the MNR moved rapidly to grant the universal vote, as we have seen, at least opening the door to Quechua and Aymará campesinos, who had been totally marginalized, locked into a history not of their making, trapped as "the majority as minority."

Secondly, nationalization of the major tin mines was next on the agenda by Paz Estenssoro, major architect of the MNR and denied the presidency by the old guard in the election of 1951, who was overwhelmingly chosen President by the people in the first test of the universal vote in 1952, a free election with wide participation (newspaper photographs of the time show campesinos lined up for blocks and blocks waiting to cast their colored ballots for the illiterate).

I first met Victor Paz Estensoro in 1968 when he was in exile in Lima. An economist, he looked more like a professor (which he was) or businessman than a revolutionary, with precise metal-rimmed glasses and austere manners. Yet he was the overriding figure of the Bolivian National Revolution for decades. I met him in his tiny office at a polytechnic institute where he was teaching to make ends meet while in exile in Lima. He had been overthrown in 1964 while embarked on his third term by General René Barrientos, his vice-president chosen to placate the military.

ARMANDO ARCE, STREET FIGHTER

The third member of the literary and journalistic triumvirate of the early MNR was Armando Arce, a less well known figure of Bolivian journalism. Arce was born into a comfortable family but was defrauded of his patrimony by his guardian after the death of his father. With a high school diploma, Armando Arce became a journalist and worked for eleven years on *El Diario*, for which Montenegro and Céspedes also once reported, becoming editor-in-chief. He left that position voluntarily to found *El Universal*, an independent daily which under his leadership was the first to launch vigorous campaigns for social and economic reform. Both Montenegro and Céspedes contributed to this newspaper during its three years of life (1932–1935) against enormous odds. It was closed by the government. Then, after a year's interval, Arce and Céspedes founded *La Calle*, dedicated to continuing the struggle against the power of the great mine owners and large landholders.

The MNR after 1941 disclaimed any official connection with *La Calle*, the gutter scrapper tabloid of La Paz journalism, but it was clearly that party's spokesman. Its name (The Street) signaled its editorial policy. In Spanish American culture, houses are places of safety and retreat, built solidly and flush against the street, which is a trafficway of persons and of ideas, a place of potential danger. Thus, the MNR announced that it would carry its fight to the streets against the entrenched enclaves of *la rosca*.

La Calle was constantly at the throats of its journalistic opponents in La Paz. It never identified them by name but referred instead to "the morning daily of the great mining interests [*La Razón*]"; the "plutocratic press" or "*la prensa rosquera*," and "the press that serves the interests of the mining superstate." On one occasion, *La Calle* derided "the hoarse cry of that venal press, traitorous to the sacred interests of the country, [which] has become converted into the strident croak of fat frogs on the point of bursting." Edited by Armando Arce throughout its stormy existence (1936–1943), *La Calle* was willing to seize upon any issue, including exploitation of the anti-Semitism latent in Bolivian life, to boost the MNR to power. *La Calle* suffered police harassment and temporary closures. Arce was jailed on several occasions.

Oscar Delgado has written a biography of Arce which asserts that as editor of both *El Universal* and *La Calle* the journalist was in "elbow-to-elbow" contact with Paz Estenssoro, who served Bolivia three times as president, and with the group of independent deputies who later formed the MNR and made Paz its leader. The latter group included Hernán Siles Zuazo, second-in-command of the MNR and president from 1956 to 1960 while Paz Estenssoro was ambassador to England. An editor of *La Nación*, Hugo González Rioja, has noted that Arce "perhaps did not foresee that what happened almost fatally to every Bolivian intellectual would happen to him: he would wind up in the political jousting field." After the victory of 1952, Arce was Bolivian ambassador to Colombia, Peru and Mexico.

At first, the group that was to form the MNR relied on reform-minded military elements as the only practical way to gain power. These men supported the tentative reforms of Colonel Germán Busch (1937–1939) before finally sharing power with Major Gualberto Villarroel (1943–1946). During this bitter period of jockeying for power, the MNR propagandists had to fight the entrenched and socially conservative press of La Paz, especially *La Razón*, the organ of tin tycoon Carlos Victor Aramayo. After the MNR gained power in 1952, the party kept *La Razón* closed, just as those who came later almost absorbed *El Diario* in 1971.

THE BOLIVIAN PRESS AND THE MNR REVOLUTION

"Our purpose was simple. It was to facilitate, through the press, the attainment of the objectives for which we were fighting. In other words, it was an attempt to enlist the help of the press for our revolution." (Victor Paz Estenssoro, President of Bolivia, speaking before the National Press Club in Washington in 1963.)

The Bolivian National Revolution would not have succeeded if the MNR had not aroused and sustained the social conscience of the thin middle sector through newspapers and literature. As *La Nación*, official newspaper spokesman of the revolution for twelve years, once declared:

"Traditionally, the MNR is a party of journalists. The founding staff was [in 1941] almost totally composed of newspapermen who marked the awakening of the conscience of the Bolivian majorities from that memorable nucleus of revolutionary thought that was *La Calle* [a daily founded in 1936]. As the years passed, those men occupied high functions in the government and in diplomacy, but almost always as a consequence of their activity displayed in the press."

Guillermo Lora, leader of the Trotskyite *Partido Obrero Revolucionario* (POR, Revolutionary Worker Party), has phrased this in an even more emphatic way, entitling a still unpublished manuscript about the MNR, "From a propaganda group, to a party of masses."

Journalism and literature are more frequently intertwined in Latin American than elsewhere in the world, and the younger Bolivian men of letters used both to wage their own war of protest. As *La Nación* noted later, "It was said in the United States about the MNR that its was a revolution without books, as it was also said of certain other countries that theirs were books without revolutions." This might have referred to neighboring Peru, where the Marxist-oriented José Carlos Mariátegui had issued a call for revolution in 1928 with his famous *Siete ensayos de interpretación de la realidad peruana* (Seven Interpretive Essays on Peruvian Reality). Yet Peru experienced no profound social change until the populist, technocratic revolution of General Juan Velasco Alvarado began in 1968.

The Bolivian press was caught in the crossfire of the Bolivian National Revolution. Those arguing for a socially committed press, had taken to heart the admonition of Pope John XXIII that the capitalist press or news services were unable or unwilling to present an accurate picture of the under-developed or non-developed countries, still in semi-colonial dependency on the industrialized north.

The case of La Razon of La Paz was never settled to the owner's or IAPA's satisfaction. But the violence which closed *Los Tiempos* of Cochabamba on November 8, 1953, was even more controversial. Founded by large landowner Demetrio Canelas on September 16, 1943, *Los Tiempos* had survived the beginning of the MNR Revolution by 19 months, even though Canelas had fought the MNR reforms, especially agrarian reform, every inch of the way.

Lee Hills former president of the IAPA, gave this version in 1969 of what happened: "The late Demetrio Canelas, of *Los Tiempos* Cochabamba, Bolivia, saw his newspaper destroyed by government-inspired mobs, and then he was thrown in prison and threatened with execution as a traitor for not bowing editorially to the government. IAPA protests saved him."

From my own interviews in Cochabamba in 1968, there was never any threat to the life of Demetrio Canelas. He was deported and allowed to return to Bolivia later, when he sought damages—never awarded—for the destruction of some of his newspaper equipment. A contemporary account of the incident by the MNR correspondent in Cochabamba, which follows, bears repeating.

The MNR spokesman *La Nación* gave quite a different account in 1959, relying on a dispatch from Cochabamba by its correspondent Julián Cayo. This newsman, sifting the evidence six years after the event, reported that *Los Tiempos* had not been "destroyed" at all. Two line casting machines were not injured while a third and the press itself were damaged only slightly and were functional again after light repairs. In fact, Canelas' "destroyed" press was first sold to *Crítica* of Cochabamba, then to *Crónica* of the same city, and finally to *Progreso* of Santa Cruz, where it continued in service.

Cayo reconstructed the events of November 9, 1953. That morning, he said, the people of Cochabamba were told by radio that a counter-revolution led by the FSB had broken out in their city. The rebels used the *Los Tiempos* building as their citadel. After the noon hour, the plant of *Los Tiempos* was taken by MNR-controlled students against machine-gun fire from the building. The students were about to issue the first issue of *El Proletario* when mobs of *campesinos* invaded and occupied the building. On November 10 the student group, *Avanzada Universitaria*, again gained control of the building for four hours. It was they who reported that the equipment had been damaged only lightly. Some 50 workers lost their lives putting down the attempted counter-revolt.

The MNR correspondent found it ironic that Canelas had used illiterate peons to carry his editorials from his nearby estate of Pucara to Cochabamba. They were "innocent porters of editorials which argued that it was necessary to perpetuate the order of a powerful bossism." Cayo charged that Canelas had conspired openly with the Rural Federation of Landowners to bring about the attempted counter-revolt of November 9, 1953, charging that the publisher had no social conscience whatsoever. He had used *pongos* (serfs) both in his country house and in the plant of *Los Tiempos* itself, where they could be seen "running like souls in pain to fulfill the domestic commands of the *patrón*." The MNR writer concluded, "dressed in coarse flannel, wearing sandals, the *campesinos* watched terrified the operation of the Linotypes and the press which was publishing the newspaper that was inciting repression of the agrarian revolution underway."

Publishing, a chronically depressed economic activity in Latin America, presented a greater challenge. With an unstable political climate and relatively few readers, book press runs had been notoriously small. For example, Carlos Montenegro's *Nacionalismo y coloniaje*, the bellwether of the revolution, had appeared in two editions of only 1,000 copies each. Under the stimulus of the revolution, however, young Alfonso Tejerina founded a publishing house that issued Fellmann Velarde's biography, *Victor Paz Estenssoro: el hombre y la revolución*, in two editions totaling 40,000 copies that sold out completely.

When Torres was in command, a conference on "Press and Revolution" was held in Cochabamba in July 1971 where many of the earlier ideas of socially committed writing first voiced in Bolivia by Montenegro and Céspedes were heard once again.

At that meeting, Alberto Bailey Gutiérrez, former head of the refashioned Ministry of Culture, Information and Tourism, declared that all means of communication within the country should be made into cooperatives to counteract the "capitalist trap imposed on the press," which separated ownership from the creative functions.

Desire to join in the national revolutionary cause was evident in other circles as well. The First Encounter of Committed Poets, held in Oruro in July 1971, issued a manifesto: "We the poets, who have gathered our song from the drama of the people, . . . are one with the proletariat, vanguard of the revolution, to assist with our art the battle of the Bolivian people for national liberation and the implantation of socialism." And a group of historians in La Paz refused to attend the second Congress of Bolivian Historians scheduled for Sucre in October 1971 unless the meeting's agenda were changed from a mere consideration of preserving national documents. Their protest stated: "To limit the Congress to the framework of mere archivism would mean that it has adopted a reactionary position at the margin of present Bolivian life. The scholar in general and historian in particular can in no way remain locked in a kind of marble tower not confronting national problems." Congress planners responded dryly, "Study of the great national problems cannot be done by memory." (*Journalism Monographs*, No. 34 (November 1973), 1–48.)

In our interview, I asked Paz Estenssoro about alleged political prisoners in Bolivia after 1952, and angrily he demanded, "Isn't the agrarian reform worth 600 political prisoners?" I then brought up the matter of *La Razón*, the newspaper of tin magnate Carlos Victor Aramayo, which had opposed every proposed reform of its day. Angry mobs after the April 1952 revolt prevented the newspaper from reopening, and the MNR government refused police protection, causing hemispheric publishers to rail against this violation of "freedom of the press." *La Razón* never reappeared, consigned to the archives by a revolution it had never understood. Paz Estenssoro in my Lima interview was furious that I brought this matter up, actually chasing me out of his office, shouting, "I refused to shoot the people to protect the property of Aramayo."

The extent of the third great postulate of the MNR Revolution, agrarian reform, has been perhaps the most controversial. Actually, the MNR program as outlined in their goals of 1941, appealed to labor and the thin middle class, scarcely mentioning the plight of landless campesinos. It was the outbreak of campesino uprisings in the Cochabamba valley after 1952, terrifying resident landlords who appealed to the United States for protection, which forced agrarian reform onto the MNR agenda.

Edward J. Sparks, later United States ambassador to Bolivia, who witnessed the promulgation of the agrarian reform decree in 1953 at Ucareña, cradle of the agrarian revolt, later described the event in a letter to me (June 30, 1974) in which he recalled that the massed 50,000 campesinos who had come to witness the event, were silent and passive when the decree was first read in Spanish but sent up a mighty roar when it was read in Quechua.

Actually, how much land was redistributed to formerly landless campesinos, mainly in the Cochabamba valley, is questionable. Augusto Céspedes wrote in a pamphlet for the Pan American Union (published in 1962), that during the first eight years of the MNR Revolution, 142,725 property titles had been distributed (p. 27).

Paz Estenssoro, back in power, in a later interview in La Paz (August 11, 1973) considered the agrarian reform, which some scholars minimize, as the greatest achievement of the Revolution. "It brought many of the campesinos into the money market for the first time," he said, "which in turn led to gradual political participation." The first things campesinos bought with their small agricultural surplus were bicycles and transistor radios (at least one station broadcast in Quechua), and one could see them pedaling along on the flat *altiplano*, headphones clamped on, bridging the chasm between two cultures.

In the 1973 interview, Paz declared the biggest mistake of the Revolution was resurrecting the armed forces, reduced from 20,000 to 3,000 during his first term in office, but rebuilt with United States aid and encouragement, under Hernán Siles, second MNR president (1956–1960) who was fearful of armed campesino militias formed to protect their land. Policy makers in the United States had the strange idea that military aid to Latin America during the Cold War would stave off the perceived Communist threat. In reality, such aid tended to arm dictators against their own people. (Both Barrientos and his successor Alfredo Ovando Candia received military training in the United States.)

Spanish and Spanish-American culture has never embraced the legal concept of military subordination to civilian rule. Opponents saw the military as "predatory," military officers bent on personal power, but defenders saw it as the "tutelary" institution which was the final arbiter in all matters concerning Bolivia.

One of my Bolivian exchange students at the University of Kentucky, Jay Aparicio, who urged me to go to Bolivia, was in La Paz when I first visited in 1968 and wangled an interview for me with Barrientos. The interview took place in a plush suburban residence. Barrientos appeared, a man then in his late 40s, wearing a dark blue suit (no uniform since his rule had been legitimized by the election of 1966, monitored by the Organization of American States). He was a handsome man, dark eyes flashing as he recited the litany of events leading up to his overthrow of Pax Estenssoro and the MNR in 1964, not because of *personalismo* (continuing in office, as Paz had embarked on his third term), Barrientos maintained, but because he found the MNR had degenerated into incompetence and corruption. (This seemed strange to me, since when I had first interviewed Paz in Lima in 1968, he was teaching at a polytechnic school on a slim salary. Apparently, not much of the Bolivian treasury had rubbed off on Paz Estenssoro.)

During the interview, Barrientos, a consummate politician, seemed more intent on impressing my Bolivian student—a potential voter—than me, the gringo professor. He was a showman of the first order, speaking fluent Quechua, and barn storming the country in his light aircraft, keeping in touch with the campesinos to offset the still powerful miners, dropping in on weddings and funerals and civic ceremonies of all kinds. Barrientos became a popular hero. He also paid large amounts of money to public relations firms in the United States (as Fulgencio Batista had done in Cuba) to bolster his image.

As part of his public relations, Barrientos started a Civic Action program, putting soldiers to work on infrastructure projects, most of which never got beyond the drawing board. Increasing armed clashes between government troops and miners culminated in the bloody massacre of San Juan on June 23, 1965, the worst since the Catavi massacre of 1941. Yet in some American accounts, Barrientos still gets good marks.

It was easy to see why he, every inch a soldier, appealed to United States military colleagues assigned to Latin America. To form a political base, Barrientos tried to forge a Campesino-Military pact. This effort seems to have had no success except perhaps in the Cochabamba Valley, scene of the major agrarian reform and the home state of Barrientos.

When the interview was over, the general embraced my Bolivian student and saluted me. Just a few months later while visiting a village, he was to die in a helicopter crash, still unknown whether accidental or political sabotage, but the Bolivian writer and MNR militant Augusto Céspedes, who spent a good part of his life representing mining districts as a deputy in the Bolivian Congress, called that helicopter crash, "providential."

A TORMENTED PAST

Bolivians have a rich—and still largely unknown pre-Spanish past except for the Inca empire which stretched from present Ecuador to mid-Chile, a well-ordered and humane civilization. Perhaps because of its sheer extent, the Inca empire later fell into warring factions. The Quechua overran the Aymará in the invasions of 1440 and 1475, and the Spanish defeated both in 1535.

The Aymará language, spoken by about one million Bolivians, is more lyrical than the gutteral Quechua, native tongue for about 18 million South

Americans. Ruth Stephan notes that the Quechua language, which derives from the court language of the Incas, is spoken more extensively now than at the end of the Inca reign in the sixteenth century.

With a young *cholo* instructor, I tried my hand at learning a few useful Quechua phrases. I would pose a question in Spanish, and he would tell me how to say it in Quechua. We were getting along fine until I asked, picturing myself stranded on the *altiplano*, "Do you have a truck?" My instructor looked at me aghast. "You can't say that," he shouted. "Those people don't have trucks!"

Three centuries of Spanish rule destroyed the complex social organization of both the Quechua and Aymará peoples. Indians were parceled out as forced laborers in the mines under the *mita* system, or as wards to be Christianized while serving as a labor force by the Spanish under the *encomienda* system (grants of Indians). After 1650, land titles were distributed openly by the Crown apart from the *encomiendas*. As the latter system declined and ultimately disappeared in the 18th century, private haciendas flourished, which exploited the Indians more severely. After Bolivia obtained its independence from Spain in 1825, the Indian communities lost even the slight protection they had received from the Crown, and the great estates steadily encroached upon Indian lands. Thus, by 1953—the time of the MNR agrarian reform—only 3,783 free campesino communities remained in the entire country—as large as Spain and France combined.

Today Bolivia is only about half its original size when it gained independence. The country lost its outlet to the sea in the War of the Pacific (1879–1883) when Bolivia and its ally Peru were roundly defeated by Chile. Bolivia lost more territory (about 20,000 square kilometers) in the Chaco War, and bartered away fringes of its patrimony to neighbors in corrupt or questionable diplomatic deals.

The central location of Bolivia in the heart of South America, bordering on five other countries, entranced Che Guevara in 1967 who hoped to use Bolivia as a launching pad to spread guerrilla warfare throughout the continent. He failed to realize that Bolivia was not Cuba, in its beginnings supported by the middle-class against a tyrannical dictator, Fulgencio Batista, both elements lacking in Bolivia. Moreover, as many have pointed out, Che Guevara and his pitiful band of 51 guerrilla fighters from Cuba and Argentina—where Indians had been decimated long ago—did not understand the mindset of Bolivian Indians, expected to rise up and rally to Che's banner, but who were suspicious of any cause which might threaten their already marginal existence. Thus, they utterly ignored or betrayed the presence of these strangers in their land.

After independence from Spain in 1825, it was not until 1918 when Gustavo A. Navarro [pen-name Tristán Marof] first brought the plight of Bolivia's native peoples to the attention of city dwellers with his book, *Renacimiento del Alto Perú* (Rebirth of Bolivia), followed by some 25 books and pamphlets on this theme, the passion of this neglected writer.

The first Indian congress, attended by about one thousand campesinos, was held during the reform interlude of Gualberto Villarroel (1943–1946) in which three MNR members participated in his cabinet. The congress recommended that education be based on Indian culture and needs rather than European or United States models, and sought to eliminate *pongueueaje* or compulsory personal service for those who owned them, but neither reform took root. In fact, newspapers of the time showed photographs of the feet of campesinos shackled so they could not escape from their workplaces.

The somewhat ruthless tactics of Villarroel provoked a mob to shoot him in the National Palace and then hang his corpse on a lamppost outside. Today that lamppost is a national monument, since Villarroel is considered a precursor to the MNR, with two honor guards in full uniform standing beside it. Some American tourists once asked me why those soldiers were standing by a lamppost. When I told them, with great relish, they shuddered and beat a hasty retreat.

THE GOOD SOLDIER: ANTONIO ARGÜEDAS AND THE BOLIVIAN DIARIES OF CHE GUEVARA

Antonio Argüedas, the high Bolivian official who sent the guerilla diaries of Che Guevara to Cuba in 1968, became a celebrity praised by some and despised by others. He died a forgotten and controversial man, gunned down on the streets of La Paz in February 2000—in the second and fatal attempt on his life. He left historians in a quandary over why Argüedas, Minister of Government, the second most powerful man in the Bolivian government, would mail Che's diaries, damaging to the Bolivian military who had captured and executed Che Guevara in the rugged terrain and rain forest of southeastern Bolivia in 1967. The military also feared that Che's account of his incursion onto their national territory, although ultimately a dismal failure, might inspire guerrilla attempts elsewhere on the continent.

They had cause for alarm. Che's band of 51 guerrillas, mainly Cubans, had joined the group at their base camp in the isolated rain forest of southeastern Bolivia after flying into El Alto airport at La Paz in twos and threes since 1966 to avoid detection. This motley crew, once assembled, had been able to elude about 5,000 Bolivian troops—trained by a small contingent of Green Berets and advised by CIA agents—for more than a year. Also, the La Paz government of President René Barrientos, a close friend of Argüedas, was well aware of the overwhelming splash the diaries would create in the world press if they got out.

The capture and summary execution of Che on October 11, 1967, created a firestorm, causing publishers to clamor for printing rights to the diaries, exposing what was considered CIA penetration of Bolivia, and forcing Argüedas to flee the country after President Barrientos had accused him as the source of the leak." Argüedas himself had served in the Air Force, where in fact he had become close friends with Barrientos, but in the view of many Bolivians he had betrayed his country. By sending a copy of the diaries to Havana, wher it was printed in *Granma*, the Communist Party newspaper, before being spread globally by the world press, Argüedas ignited the fierce Bolivian national pride. This sentiment is especially strong in the smaller or weaker Latin American countries, perhaps because it is a diversion from their poverty and other problems.

The diaries, two small notebooks which Che—an inveterate diary keeper-always carried with him were not great literature. Nor did they add anything to guerrilla warfare tactics not covered in his *Guerrilla Warfare* published in New York in 1961. They were simply the matter-of-fact daily record of a celebrated political figure bent on an impossible quest. Thus, publication of his final diaries and the circumstances of his death aroused enormous interest and added to Che's legendary martyrdom.

As one Bolivian Army officer put it, "Che Guevara, in death, has hurt us far more than he ever could as a guerrilla." After the final skirmish, Che's live body with five bullet wounds was helicoptered to the little thatched schoolhouse at La Higuera where he was shot two days later. While the body was being photographed, a CIA employee, Félix Ramos Rodríguez, microfilmed the brief diaries.

The highest Bolivian officials in La Paz feared the adverse international publicity of a trial for Che Guevara, recalling that of Regis Debray, the French revolutionary dilettante who had attached himself to Che and had been captured earlier along with his Argentine companion, Ciro Roberto Bustos. Thus, those in command in La Paz radioed their subordinates at La Higuera to execute Che immediately. To justify their position, the "Armed Forced Communique to Close the Record on Che's Death," issued on October 16, 1967, stated flatly that Che "died as a result of his injuries." (The La Paz newspapers also had been reporting that Che died in battle).

It was an inglorious end for the hero of the battle of Santa Clara, a turning point in the Cuban Revolution which ended the oppression of the dictator Fulgencio Batista in 1959 and made Che the poster boy of the Cuban Revolution, later touring Socialist countries and speaking before such assemblies as the Organization of American States and the United Nations.

He surfaced briefly in 1965, leading about 200 Cuban troops with the Kenshasa rebels in the Congo. They failed totally, and Che returned to Cuba where, although an Argentine, he had been made a Cuban citizen. Bored with his position as Minister of Finance, which included agrarian reform, Che turned to Bolivia in the interior of South America and bordering on five countries, hoping to make this central country a base to become "the Vietnam of America."

But Che's excursion into Bolivia, as the diaries reveal, failed because he did not realize that Bolivia was not Cuba, which had a largely white middle class population opposing a hated dictator. Bolivia, on the other hand, was about 60 percent Indian, whether Quechua or Aymar, living a marginal existence at best, who would not risk what little they had to flock to Che's banner as expected. They also distrusted strangers. Jorge Castaneda, for example, described Che as a man who looked at peasant populations "and saw people ripe for revolution, while they looked at him, and saw and eccentric, threatening intruder."

Amidst popular unrest over the diaries slipping through the fingers of the Bolivian military, Barrientos declared on July 19, 1968 that Antonio Argüedas, his second-in-command, had betrayed his country by sending Che's Bolivian diaries to Cuba. Historians have pondered ever since why he did it. Henry Butterfield Ryan, for example, wrote: "Clearly, Argüedas had plenty of potential reasons to send the diaries to Fidel Castro [revenge against the CIA, for example, whom he claimed had forced him into their service], but why he did so remains a mystery." An extensive biography by Jon Lee Anderson skirts the issue, stating "inexplicably [Argüedas] refound his Marxist leanings in 1968… and in a mystifying series of about-faces he later left Cuba." (He was never in Cuba except for a courtesy visit of a few days in Havana.) Richard L. Harris wrote, "the Cuban government mysteriously obtained a copy and released it through a series of publishing houses in Latin America, Europe, and the United States," Daniel James' early biography claims that Argüedas, when he sent the diaries to Castro, "confessed that he held the same revolutionary beliefs as Castro and Guevara."

But in the recently published *Motorcycle Diaries*, Che's traveling companion, Alberto Granados, reveals that Che, 23 years old then, was not a Marxist at that time but he was radicalized by the halfway reforms they witnessed in Bolivia and Guatemala. As a young man, Antonio Argüedas was briefly a member of the Bolivian Communist Party, which was never very strong, despite assumptions to the contrary, because small nationalist revolutionary parties siphoned off possible members. Yet all sorts of erratic behavior, political and otherwise, dogged Argüedas. As Richard L. Harris has pointed out, the CIA "has successfully planted a considerable amount of information in the Bolivian and Latin American press that depicted Argüedas as either a traitor or a madman."

On June 30, 1968, Che's Bolivian diaries appeared in *Granma*, the spokesman for the Cuban Communist Party. In a speech the night before, Castro declared, "The manner in which this diary came into our hands cannot yet be revealed; let it suffice that this was done without the slightest financial remuneration." Aleida March, the widow of Che, had helped with his difficult handwriting. The Cuban press run was an unprecedented 600,000 freely distributed, with the printers aiming for one million. The diaries also were translated and published in *Punto Final* of Chile, in France by the editorial Francois Masquero, in Italy by the publishers of Feltronelli, and in West Germany by Trikent Vrtlag.

Anxious for book rights, the first publisher representative on the scene was the French journalist, Michele Ray, representing *Paris Match*, who flew to La Paz to get exclusive rights to publish the diaries. Learning that the Bolivian military—once the diaries had become public—had a standing price of $200,000 to publish them, she made a bogus counter offer of $400,000. She told General Alfredo Ovando Candia, chief of staff of the Army, that "the diaries in the United States [would be] like the Koran in the hands of the infidels." Eventually, Orlando realized that the $400,000 was a phantom offer, and the deal fell through.

Next in line was the venerable *New York Times*, which dispatched Juan de Onis, longtime specialist in Latin American affairs. But he found so many obstacles that he cabled his boss that the Bolivians guarded the diary [at that time] as though it were the Dead Sea Scrolls.

Ramparts, the radical West Coast magazine, first actually published the diaries in the United States on July 3, 1968, with the famous Christ-like photograph of Che on the cover. It was a literary and popular sensation. *Ramparts* also made arrangements to publish the diaries for wider distribution through Bantam Books.

The first book version in the United States was put out by the publishing house of Stein and Day, apparently with CIA backing. Naively, the motive seems to have been to distribute as widely as possible Che's diaries as a warning or cautionary tale of the ultimate fate of guerrillas everywhere. *Ramparts* exulted in a headline and story, THE CIA FINDS A PUBLISHER. As Henry Butterfield Ryan, retired U.S. Foreign Service officer and historian, has commented, "Can one doubt that the U.S. government and probably the CIA, helped Stein and Day to obtain the diaries?"

Bolivians were not uninformed about the contents of Che's diaries, however. The newspaper *Presencia*, a commercial Catholic daily of substantial circulation in La Paz, monitored the text broadcast from the radio La Cubana of Havana and processed in the studios of Radio Méndez. The diaries were printed in *Presencia* on July 7, 1967 with Che's entries from the beginnings of the guerrilla movement on March 23, 1966 to several days before his death. This issue of *Presencia* provoked riots in the streets of La Paz, defending Bolivian sovereignty. The toll of the riots—a police captain killed, five wounded and numerous arrests, while the more orderly lined up for blocks to see what Che had to say.

More importantly, Bolivians wanted to know how the diaries escaped from government safekeeping. The original and microfilms were supposedly in the hands of the military, regarded as the "tutelary" body charged with safekeeping the nation and its honor. One copy, however, went to the office of Antonio Argüedas, Minister of Government (and conveniently a civilian). The military sought frantically to protect the prestige of the Armed Forces, who didn't crush Che's rebellion earlier and also let the diaries slip through their hands.

In my interview with Barrientos in La Paz on July 1, 1968, he recited the litany of events leading up to the MNR (Movimiento Nacionalista Revolucionario) Nationalist Revolutionary Movement which gained power in 1952, and justified his role in overthrowing it in 1964 because it had become "a revolution only on paper." None of us knew that within a year the charismatic Barrientos would die in a helicopter crash that some say was an accident and others, sabotage. Augusto Céspedes, Bolivia's best known writer and long-time MNR militant until his death in 1995, declared that the helicopter crash was "providential" after Barrientos' maltreatment of miners culminating in the Massacre of San Juan of 1961.

Argüedas, close friend of Barrientos, was the pivotal figure in this unfolding drama. When Argüedas earned a law degree, Barrientos appointed him Minister of Government after the overthrow of the MNR in 1963. Argüedas served his friend as number-two man in the government for twenty-three months.

Biographers of Che Guevara have made much of Argüedas' checkered or erratic political career, perhaps based on the false information distributed by the CIA which Harris has cited, or perhaps simply that of a young man in search of an ideology. He never found one, although he was briefly affiliated with the Bolivian Communist Party in 1951, which was never very strong (despite the assumptions of some writers who make much of the refusal of Mario Monje, head of the PCB in La Paz to support the Guevara venture) because numerous nationalist revolutionary political parties siphoned off members, but this did not seem to bother Barrientos. He considered his young friend a "nationalist and [Bolivian] revolutionary."

Two men with such divergent political views—Barrientos conservative, and Argüedas radical—could still be close friends and work together, even mountain climb together. Argüedas had been a member of the MNR, but he shared Barrientos' view that the movement had become *personalista* after the universal vote had been granted in 1952 and Victor Paz Estenssoro, the MNR leader, insisted on running for a third term in 1964.

Argüedas was later elected deputy in the National Left Revolutionary Party (PRIN) headed by the durable labor leader Juan Lechín. As a colleague sums it up, "God knows what cause [Argüedas embraced] but there is no doubt that he was protected by President Barrientos."

Before the storm of controversy over Che's diaries broke, Argüedas lived a comfortable, middle-class life with his wife and three children in a suburb of La Paz. It was said that Edward Fox, the Air Force attaché at the U.S. Embassy, could not tolerate a former Communist [Argüedas] in the Bolivian government. Fox exceeded his authority, but allegedly warned Argüedas that if he did not resign, the United States would cut off all aid to Bolivia [Fox later denied this]. Argüedas did resign, but two weeks later the CIA offered his job back if he would do assignments for them while serving as Minister of Government. Argüedas agreed (his motives unknown, but in a sense he was blackmailed). Perhaps he also wanted to know—from the inside out—the extent of CIA penetration of his country. To insure his loyalty, the CIA sent Argüedas off to a three-day "orientation" session in Lima.

After Barrientos blamed Argüedas for the sudden disappearance of the diaries from La Paz and their appearance on the pages of *Granma*, an enterprising reporter from *El Diario* staked out Barrientos' house and kept a time-table on Thursday, July 18, 1968. The Armed Forces chiefs met there to discuss the matter of the diaries at 3 p.m., and Alfredo Ovando Candia, head of the Army, ended their deliberations at 7 p.m. At 10 p.m. Barrientos called Argüedas and said he wanted to talk to him.

After that meeting, at 10:15 p.m. Argüedas and his brother Jaime fled in a jeep belonging to the Ministry of Government for the arduous seven-hour trip to the Chilean border, where they hoped to get political asylum. Interned briefly at Calchanes, Chile, the two were later transported to the nearest airport at Iquique. When they arrived at Santiago, there were more crowds greeting Argüedas than came to see the arriving Galo Plaza, secretary general of the Organization of American States.

Argüedas request for political asylum was refused because Bolivia and Chile had broken diplomatic relations during the Rio Lauca dispute in the north in 1961. Also, if there were extradition proceedings, it would mean that Chile would in effect judge Argüedas, a purely Bolivian matter, before handing him over. Then Bolivia tried to extradite Argüedas through neutral Brazil, but that too failed, and Argentina also refused to accept him. Antonio Argüedas had become "a man without a country."

Finally, Argüedas admitted that he had mailed a micro-film copy of the diaries to Cuba on June 12, 1968, "a unilateral action." When some Bolivians suggested that the remains of Che Guevara be exchanged for Bolivian prisoners in Cuban jails, Barrientos replied, "We have almost forgotten the incident."

When asked by a Peruvian policeman why Argüedas gave the diaries to Cuba, Argüedas replied that he wanted to see them in print before the CIA could doctor them, "which might implicate others." Followed by CIA agents, Argüedas made a whirlwind tour through Santiago, London, New York and Lima blasting the CIA wherever he went. Most scholars believe Argüedas was right about the operations within the Bolivian government by the CIA, although his observations were exaggerated. At home, a headline in the official n ewspaper *La Nación* called his performance "A lamentable spectacle that Bolivia does not deserve."

One journalist asked him why he was going to London and New York, and he replied, "to strike the imperialists on their own ground." At the same time, the Barrientos government offered the olive branch for Argüedas to come home and be judged by his fellow countrymen.

But there were too many things unexplained. Argüedas had left the residence of Barrientos on the night of July 18, 1968 with his brother headed for Chile. Why, if he were a traitor to his country, would Barrientos let him go? The jeep headed for the Chilean border had to pass police check-points every 20 or 30 kilometers without once being stopped.

Antonio Argüedas was the sacrificial lamb for the Bolivian Army and his friend René Barrientos. He abandoned his family and his career for what he perceived to be the best for Bolivia—the integrity of the Bolivian Armed Forces. He didn't care a fig for the Cuban Revolution. He never visited Cuba except once for ceremonial purposes, even when Chancellor Raul Roa offered him asylum and crowds cheered him at the Havana airport.

Presencia reported what everyone else had missed—the widespread rumor in the Chilean news media that the whole Argüedas affair was a "political show" cooked up by Barrientos and Ovando to take the heat off the Bolivian Army. *El Diario's* reporter in Santiago wrote:

> The Chilean police and other officials cannot hide the impression that the flight of Argüedas was planned by the Bolivian government to eliminate all suspicion [against the] Army in the `affaire' of [Che's] campaign.

In the small Damasco hotel in Lima in August 1968 where Argüedas had taken refuge from the crowds of reporters looking for him at the major hotels on his way back to Bolivia in August 1968, I interviewed him. One of his bodyguards wanted to bar me from seeing him because "Argüedas does not grant individual interviews to avoid showing favoritism." But the bodyguard accepted my credentials as a historian and I soon met Antonio Argüedas, an intense man about forty, who seemed completely in control of the situation. He also struck me as both intelligent and perfectly aware of what he was doing. Argüedas was a Bolivian first and "the good soldier" second, sacrificing his own career for what he perceived the greater good of his country. His own ideology was nationalism, perhaps the strongest—and at times most destructive—force abroad in the world in the 20th and 21st centuries. Here are key excerpts of one of the voices we seldom hear:

Question: Some Bolivians speculate that giving Che Guevara's diaries to Cuba, which would eventually have wound up there anyway, and your subsequent travels attacking the CIA have been a "political farce" staged by the government of President Barrientos to protect the prestige of the Bolivian Armed Forces.

Answer: The Bolivian people do not believe this. Only the CIA, with its paid press, has disseminated such rumors. To keep the propaganda mill going, there was one CIA agent with me constantly in Santiago and London, and two in New York.

Question: You have been quoted many times as referring to "United States imperialism." Exactly what do you mean by that phrase? Are you referring to corporate enterprises such as Gulf Oil or the government of the United States?

Answer: Not Gulf, not private United States enterprises. I was Minister of Government when the contracts with Gulf and other firms were concluded. If the Bolivian people judge these contracts to be wrong, they must judge me to have been wrong. By imperialism, I refer to the government of the United States and especially to the CIA which runs Bolivia like a puppet.

[He charged that the CIA had used him to bribe and corrupt Bolivian government officials to carry out United States policy in Bolivia.] "I wanted out and they wouldn't let me out," he said. "I intended all the time to return to Bolivia. It is my country."

Antonio Argüedas did return to his country on August 17, 1968 and defended himself at his own trial maintaining that since there were no military secrets contained in the diaries, he could not be convicted for treason. The court ruled that only the legislature could judge a minister of state. The Bolivian legislature never met for that purpose. After years of living in Mexico,

Argüedas returned to stay the rest of his life in Bolivia. In February 2000 he was assassinated in La Paz.

MY BOLIVIA—LAND AND PEOPLE

There are two Bolivians whom I admire most. The first is Dr. Hugo Palazzi, son of an Aymará mother and Italian father, who apparently footed the bill for his son to graduate from the Harvard College of Medicine. Dr. Palazzi had the opportunity to establish a lucrative practice anywhere in the United States, but he chose to return to Bolivia where I met him in 1968, running a one-man, two-room "clinic" in La Paz where he treated anyone who needed it.

The other person was Lydia Gueiler Tejada, a strikingly handsome woman of German descent in her mid-fifties with blonde hair, blue eyes, and a compassionate face. I first met her when she was a delegate to the Popular Assembly, and she was also a longtime Deputy in the Bolivian Congress. She was the first woman to break the barrier against her sex in national politics, where she earned the respect of her all-male colleagues so highly, they named her interim President in the deadlock following the overthrow of Torres. She made headlines in the United States press when she chased intruders bent on a coup out of her presidential bedroom, and finished the task assigned her as interim President.

My Bolivian student, along with his American wife and young son, proposed an excursion to the *yungas*, the sub-tropical valleys which slope from the mountains down to tributaries of the Amazon, to visit his grandmother in the little town of Chulumani. I do not recommend this trip to the fainthearted because of the single-track dirt road which at first clings to the side of the foothills of the Andes where little white crosses mark the spots where travelers before us had gone over the edge and plunged into the chasm below. If you meet an oncoming car or truck, one or the other, usually after some discussion of the matter, must back up to the nearest wide spot carved out for that purpose.

Chulumani itself is a lovely little subtropical town with bougainvillea cascading down the fronts of some houses, and my student filled a bag with oranges from his grandmother's backyard to take back to La Paz. She herself was confined to her bed, and while I was there a chicken wandered in and hopped up on her bed, apparently looking for a soft place to lay an egg, which she did. The grandmother, with humor, said, "That chicken has a good heart. She knows I am old and sick, and that egg is a gift of love."

The place I always wanted to visit, since childhood, was Potosí with its fabulous hill of 5,000 separate little silver mines that produced so much silver in the colonial period that prices quadrupled in Europe in the 16th century. In its heyday, Potosí had 200,000 inhabitants (46,000 in 1962) some living in beautiful colonial houses built three centuries ago. But to Augusto Céspedes, behind the romantic aura of Potosí lurked a "history of terrible sacrifice for the millions of Indians [through the years] who worked in its tunnels." (Pan American Union, p. 27).

Another pleasant day's outing was Lake Titicaca, highest navigable lake in the world. Landlocked Bolivia, believe it or not, has a Navy with a small station on the Bolivian side of the lake, along with a little settlement and marketplace. The lake itself is an incredibly deep blue color with green fringes. One can see campesinos with their hand-made balsa crafts (like gondolas) plying the waters as they have for centuries. Thor Heyerdahl hired several of these craftsmen and brought them to Norway to build RA-1 and II to test the possibility of early migration across the Atlantic, as he had demonstrated earlier in the Pacific. I have often wondered what those campesino artisans thought of their trans-Atlantic flight. I imagine they approached the experience with caution but carefully concealed enjoyment. (The Atlantic efforts failed, however, and although they took no part in the attempted crossing itself, they undoubtedly were glad to get back home.)

Libraries. God bless them and all who dwell therein. Throughout Latin America, however, public libraries are the exception rather than the rule. Those who have the means build up their own private libraries while public collections go begging. In Bolivia, for example, the books in the Municipal Library are so few that I actually made an inventory of them, about twelve typewritten pages, for my own use and that of others. When I was there during a military interlude and saw a soldier standing guard inside the Municipal Library, I asked my Bolivian companion, "What is a soldier doing in a library?" To which he replied, with a grin, "Para guardar el silencio!" (To keep the silence!)

Or a more comprehensive library was that of the Universidad Mayor de San Andrés, Bolivia's institution of highest learning. During the Torres regime and things were tense, I was working away in the library at San Andrés, when a young fellow sat down beside me and kept saying in a low voice, CIA, CIA, CIA. I ignored him and eventually he went away, but I have always wondered what he thought the CIA might glean from old Bolivian newspapers.

On a lighter note, the arrival of the first Xerox machine at the San Andrés library (remember, this was 1968) was quite an occasion. The director of the Library himself showed off his most recent acquisition and he advised the librarian, a lovely old woman, deaf as a post but eager to please, that I was to have free access to it. "Oh yes," she replied. "Sr. Xerox can use the Knudson machine whenever he wants."

A jarring note interrupted our conversation. A couple of American young-sters, backpacks and all, burst into the Library, saw the three or four cabinets which comprised the entire card catalog and said in a loud voice, "So this is their library!" I saw one of them later on the street and tried to explain why he had offended both the librarian and the students. "Fuck you!" he yelled and swaggered away.

Balancing that out was the gentle humor of the Bolivian gentleman, getting along in years, at the library in the Congress building on the Plaza Murillo, seldom tapped by American researchers since it contains only the bound vol-umes of some Bolivian newspapers. All one summer he wrestled (although I helped) these large volumes for me, sometimes from the topmost shelves on a step-ladder which had seen its better days. One day, to encourage him I announced that I would be leaving in August. "What year?" he asked.

Also in the Congress building there was a café where a young waiter in impeccable white jacket and tennis shoes served tea or coffee to the highest dignitaries of the Bolivian government, with his baby slung nonchalantly over one shoulder (apparently his wife had other things to do that afternoon). No one seemed to mind. That's Bolivia.

Otherwise, the streets of La Paz are a never-ending miracle. All Indian women wear their jaunty derby hats (the story goes that sometime in the nineteenth century a haberdashery shop owner made a mistake and ordered thousands of them. To solve his problem, he advertised in the La Paz news-papers that derby hats were all the rage for European women. The thing caught on, and to this day no Aymará or Quechua woman would be caught without one.

Others spread their newspapers on the sidewalk to attract buyers (those who can't read can always look at the pictures). They compete with the open-air book stalls at the end of the Prado, the main thoroughfare of La Paz. The vendors of these books are fascinating men to deal with. If they do not have a book, they will get it for you-at three times their stall price. And even if it were a book on the premises one must go through an elaborate process of bargaining-a kind of intellectual foreplay before the final consummation. Many times I have seen fathers bringing their young sons to these open-air book stalls on a Saturday afternoon to teach them the love of books.

And there were other incidents of the street which intrigued me. Once I passed a man stretched out on the sidewalk. Thinking him possibly in need of medical attention, I reported the incident to a soldier farther down the block (I could never tell the difference between a soldier and a policeman in Bolivia since they wear the same uniforms). The soldier snapped to attention, saluted me with the word "Caballero!" (Sir!) and took off in search of the man in need. It occurred to me later that the poor guy was probably just drunk. I hope he didn't wind up in the Panóptico Nacional or national prison where the only food you get is that which your family brings you. Even prisons in Bolivia are family oriented.

I miss La Paz. I miss that rooster in a city of one million souls, which woke me up every morning even though I lived on the seventh story of a downtown apartment building. That rooster probably belonged to a campesino who came to the city in search of work, but could not leave the countryside entirely behind.

I miss those industrious workers who weave their way among the crowds in downtown La Paz with huge slabs of raw beef on their backs, yelling "Con Permiso!" ("Make way, please!").

I miss those smiling Aymará women with their cheerful babies in tow, strapped comfortably to their mother's back. I miss the chatter of Quechua and Aymará voices in the street.

On a Sunday afternoon before I was to leave Bolivia after five summers of research there, being a romantic at heart, I decided to make the climb up the hill of Laikacota to bid farewell to the city I had come to love. It was not a steep climb but well worth it to get the sweeping view of La Paz sprawled all over the canyon below. The path was well marked with little gutters draining polluted water and raw sewage from the huts alongside it. [The hill of Laikacota, once the scene of fierce fighting by hold-outs in previous confrontations, has since been demolished to curb an unruly river below.]

Sitting and contemplating the city sprawled up and down the canyon walls, I remembered the taxi drivers who, rather than asking "What block?" will say, "What altitude?" Below me was a glittering panorama as the lights came on. And as I sat on the crest of a hill that soon would be no more, as the sun disappeared below the rim of the altiplano, I realized that a chapter of my life was closing, and I wept.

Chapter Three

Origins of the Cuban Revolution

Anyone who believes that the political landscape of Cuba will change radically now that Fidel Castro has finally relinquished control of his Revolution after a long illness may be sadly mistaken, for his social experiment in the Caribbean, unless there is foreign intervention, has long since become institutionalized, or in other words permanently established.

Americans watched with wonder and awe after a correspondent and editorial writer for the New York *Times*, Herbert L. Matthews, made his historic trek in 1957 into the foothills of the Sierra Maestra mountains on the eastern end of Cuba. He proved that Castro and some of the other 82 men aboard the ramshackle old yacht Granma who survived the disastrous attempt to breach the island fortress of dictator Fulgencio Batista, were still alive and holed up in the Sierra Maestra.

The influence of Matthews' largely laudatory three-part article in the New York *Times* on Castro and his mission has been the subject of scholarly and popular debate ever since. Latest entry is Anthony De Palma's chronicle of the Matthews interview and its aftermath, The Man Who Invented Fidel (2008), a journalistic feat which created quite a splash in the United States but—contrary to popular belief and author De Palma—had little impact in Cuba.

The Cuban Revolution actually began in 1953, four years before the Matthews' interview, with the abortive attack by Castro, then 27 years old, leading 126 rebels against the regime of General Fulgencio Batista with a suicide attack on the Moncada and Bayamo Barracks in Oriente Province, the most heavily fortified military installations in Cuba, at dawn on July 26, 1953, a date enshrined in Cuban history as the battle cry of Castro's July 26 Movement. As Celia Sanchez, who later had been with the guerrilla fighters all the way from the Sierra Maestra to Havana, summed it up, "The Cuban Revolution was born at Moncada." It was a suicide mission, perhaps engineered for its later propaganda value in the mythology of the Cuban Revolution.

In a meticulous account of this pivotal event, Antonio Rafael de la Cova, spanning three decades of interviews with surviving participants on both sides, *The Moncada Attack, Birth of the Cuban Revolution* (2007), the author "discounts the account by Fidel Castro who claimed that rebel captives had been subject to prisoner torture, mutilation, and dismemberment (xii)." Batista himself in *Cuba Betrayed* (1962) denied that he had ordered the murder of ten rebel prisoners for each soldier killed in attack (some eighteen). Marta Rojas of Bohemia, who first covered the assault and subsequent trials, belies the belief by many that Castro's trial was held in secrecy and therefore of little propaganda importance in the coming revolutionary struggle. On the contrary, news of the atrocities committed against the 70 prisoners, accurate or not, galvanized public opinion against Batista. A total of 29 other prisoners were brought to trial and sentenced up to a maximum of 30 years (Cuba had no death penalty), along with Fidel Castro, at the prison camp on the Isle of Pines, but all were released in the amnesty of 1955.

In the futile attack, some 70 rebels were captured, tortured and summarily executed. Twenty-nine others were charged with "conspiracy and armed insurrection" in a trial held October 16, 1953 in the Emergency Tribunal of Santiago de Cuba. Castro himself was not tried with the others, but in a trial open to the public and attended by six reporters. It was held separately in a large room at Civil Hospital, indicating that he was considered then not only as leader of the group but also as a greater threat to the Batista regime.

A graduate of the Law School of the University of Havana (which merits the title of Doctor in Latin America), Castro chose to defend himself. At the close of the trial, the judge asked him if he had anything to say. He did, and said it for two hours. This became his famous "Condemn me. History Will Absolve Me" speech. Historians doubt that notes for the later tract were actually written down as Castro spoke. Most likely is that Castro reconstructed it himself, undoubtedly with embellishments, whether in his jail cell or later, with perhaps changes or additions by others along the way. But it was clandestinely printed and circulated by June 3, 1954. It became the prime document of the Cuban Revolution.

At first, Americans—always for the underdog—were entranced by Castro and his growing band of guerrilla fighters whose sporadic battles against the overwhelming, but demoralized Cuban Army of dictator Fulgencio Batista, were not dramatic in themselves, except the decisive battle of Santa Clara which cut the island in two, dividing and thus weakening Batista's forces. This was the strategy of Che Guevara, whose remains are buried in a monument there after finally being released by General Juan José Torres of Bolivia in 1971. It was a long way from the Sierra Maestra to the streets of Havana, where the rebels were victoriously greeted on January 1, 1959, when Batista and his entourage fled to Miami.

In Cuba, as noted, the Matthews interview had little to do with this. One wonders if it had any real impact on United States policy toward Cuba at that time at all, as De Palma maintains, since the United States did not stop supporting the Batista regime until six months before it collapsed. At the time of my monograph, published in 1978 and presented below, it was commonly believed in the United States that Herbert L. Matthews was responsible for the Cuban Revolution, a myth resurrected by De Palma. In New York subways, mimicking a current advertising campaign, a poster showed a caricature of Castro astride the island of Cuba with the caption, "I got my job through the New York *Times*." And in the New York offices of UPI, I saw a large poster which proclaimed, "PUT CASTRO IN HIS PLACE—TAKE UPI."

Public opinion on Castro, the former hero, first soured in public opinion in the United States with the summary "trials" and execution of some 700 Batista officials or adherents in Havana stadium, but few journalists could deny that Batista's clandestine forces had probably executed some 20,000 Cubans previously without any legal safeguards. The figure of 20,000 victims of the Batista regime was arrived at by A.J. Liebling (The Press, 1961, p. 199). Americans knew little of this state terror before Castro, regarding Cuba and especially Havana as a preferred playground.

A case could well be made that Fidel Castro invented Fidel Castro. Within Cuba, he did not need Herbert Matthews to do so, as Castro's famous speech of 1953 at his trial after the abortive attack on the Moncada barracks four years before the Matthews interview, "Condemn Me. History Will Absolve Me," an attack scarcely mentioned by De Palma, amply indicates. But in reality what "invented" Fidel Castro came first from his fellow countrymen in Oriente province, promised land in the 1973 speech (see below) and others like them along the way, capped by the outrage of the middle class of the cities at the increasing brutality of the Batista regime. In one of several letters to me, answering questions put to him, Matthews, who had retired in Australia, declared, "If Castro had not been exactly as I described him [in the interview], he could not have done what he did."

All his life Matthews strived to defend the accuracy of the interview and the course of the Cuban Revolution. De Palma and others tend to dismiss these efforts, which largely have been borne out by events in Cuba, as nothing more than self-justification, but if one would discard the testimony of those who took an intimate part in events for that reason, he or she would wipe out perhaps half of all historical sources which are most meaningful.

Until recently, Americans knew very little about what was happening in Cuba, until the lingering illness of the 80-year-old leader (who suddenly became President Castro on the evening news) because of the Embargo, which didn't work because Europeans continued to trade with the island and vacation or seek medical attention there. (According to the World Health Organization, Cuba now ranks third among all world countries in delivery of health services to its people, while the United States ranks twenty-seventh). Americans are forbidden to travel to Cuba to see for themselves, while Radio Marti in Florida still aims propaganda and music to the island. Cubans reportedly enjoy the music. And London-based Amnesty International censured the United States for violation of human rights by holding prisoners indefinitely at Guantanamo without trial.

At this point (August 2008), how does one assess Fidel Castro? With the onset of his illness, power was temporarily handed over and ultimately relinquished to his brother Raul, head of the armed forces and always second-in-command. The transition seemed to be going smoothly. Initially, Castro and his men, who vowed not to shave until the dictator Fulgencio Batista was defeated, inherited distrust of the United States from the era of gunboat diplomacy in the Caribbean and Central America of earlier decades to 1965 when President Lyndon Johnson sent in the Marines to the Dominican Republic. Any remnants of the Good Neighbor policy of Franklin Delano Roosevelt or the later Alliance for Progress of John F. Kennedy were shattered.

Cubans rose to the challenge of the Bay of Pigs invasion planned by the CIA with Cuban exiles trained in Guatemala, and also survived the role of pawn in a dangerous nuclear chess game when Soviet missiles in Cuba threatened the United States in 1962 during the Cold War. In the settlement, Cuba won the pledge by the United States to no longer challenge the island's sovereignty. With the collapse of the Soviet Union later, however, Cuba lost a valuable source of external aid-estimated at one million dollars a day. (Castro had first declared himself a Marxist-Leninist in 1961, two years after gaining power.)

In the midst of this, a little volume of Fidel Castro's correspondence, "Cartas del Presidio" ("Letters from Prison") contained twenty-one revealing letters from the charismatic leader to his family and close friends. It was published in Havana by Luis Conte Aguero only months after Castro and his men overthrew the Batista regime in January 1959.

An anonymous reviewer of this collection of Castro's early letters perceptively described him: "The letters amply illustrate Castro's many gifts: his formidable erudition, strategic thinking and natural leadership. They are also an early indicator of his Machiavellian cunning and his genius for public

relations [especially his use of television]. And they dramatize his resent-
ments and rages. Castro was remorseless and unforgiving of his perceived
enemies, a man for whom compromise was a mark of weakness."

The person who compiled these letters, Luis Conte Aguero, became disil-
lusioned with the Cuban Revolution and left, along with thousands of others who had suffered loss of their property or political persecution. Every
revolution has its émigrés. Loyalists during or after the American Revolution
fled to Canada or England, leaving behind their property and American ties
established many years or generations before. The influx of French émigrés
to the United States after the French Revolution began in 1787 (a total of
about 25,000 foreigners in the United States at that time) partly triggered the
Federalist Alien and Sedition Acts (1798–1801).

Americans tend to be slow in facing reality. It took us sixteen years after
the Bolshevik Revolution in Russia in 1917 to recognize the Soviet Union,
and twenty-two years before we acknowledged the existence of the People's
Republic of China after 1948. Cuba, ninety miles off our shores, remains in
limbo since the successful Castro Revolution of 1959.

But let us re-examine the roots of the Cuban Revolution-both my account
of what was expected in the United States after the Matthews interview of
1957, written soon after the extensive (and at that time uncatalogued) Matthews papers became available at Columbia University. But more importantly
what did many Cubans expect from Fidel Castro's "History Will Absolve
Me" speech at his trial in 1953 after the attack on the Moncada Barracks, four
years before the Matthews interview?

Some historians question the immediate impact of that speech, believing
it to have become public only much later, but in reality it was clandestinely
printed and circulated by June 3, 1954, within a year after the attack on the
Moncada Barracks and subsequent trials. Word of mouth also spreads quickly
in Cuba, and the public soon learned of the atrocities-torture and summary
executions committed against the 70 rebel prisoners by orders of the Barracks
commander, Rio Chaviano. As the British historian Hugh Thomas (Cuba, or
the Pursuit of Freedom, 1971) points out:

> The consequences on public opinion of Moncada and its aftermath were consid-
> erable. Had it not been for the repression, the Moncada attack would doubtless
> have been dismissed as one more wild and semi-gangster incident in the life
> of Fidel Castro. The repression and the trial made Castro appear henceforth
> something of a hero. Professional, Catholic, liberal or middle class opinion was
> outraged (p. 843).

Castro himself at his trial fully realized that he was laying down a blueprint
for revolution and the propaganda value of what he was saying, declaring,

"This speech of high moral and idealistic value will also be printed abroad, where better printing facilities exist, and it will be distributed throughout the democracies of Latin America as an example of the courage and idealism of Cuban youth." (Robert Taber, History Will Absolve Me, 1961, p. 6).

Here, then are several cogent portions of that speech, perhaps with changes or embellishments, which became the cherished document of the Cuban Revolution. It reveals, most of all, that Castro's appeal at first was primarily not to the middle class, although it increasingly favored him as the Batista regime became more brutal, but rather to the landless farmers of Oriente province whom he hoped would join his cause.

CONDEMN ME, HISTORY WILL ABSOLVE ME

In the brief of this cause there must be recorded the five revolutionary laws that would have been proclaimed immediately after the capture of the Moncada barracks and would have been broadcast to the nation by radio. It is possible that Colonel Chaviano may deliberately have destroyed these documents, but even if he has done so, I conserve them in my memory.

The First Revolutionary Law would have returned power to the people and proclaimed the Constitution of 1940 the supreme Law of the land, until such time as the people should decide to modify or change it. And, in order to effect its implementation and punish those who had violated it—there being no organization for holding elections to accomplish this—the revolutionary movement, as the momentous incarnation of this sovereignty, the only source of legitimate power, would have assumed all the faculties inherent to it, except that of modifying the Constitution itself: In other words it would have assumed the legislative, executive and judicial powers.

This approach could not be more crystal clear nor more free of vacillation and sterile charlatanry. A government acclaimed by the mass of rebel people would be vested with every power, everything necessary in order to proceed with the effective implementation of the popular will and true justice. From that moment, the Judicial Power, which since March 10th has placed itself *against* the Constitution and *outside* the Constitution, would cease to exist and we would proceed to its immediate and total reform before it would again assume the power granted to it by the Supreme Law of the Republic. Without our first taking those previous measures, a return to legality by putting the custody of the courts back into the hands that have crippled the system so dishonorably would constitute a fraud, a deceit, and one more betrayal.

The Second Revolutionary Law would have granted property, not mortgageable and not transferable, to all planters, sub-planters, lessees, partners and squatters who hold parcels of five or less "caballerias" (tract of land, about 33⅓ acres) of land, and the state would indemnify the former owners on the basis of the rental which they would have received for these parcels over a period of ten years.

The Third Revolutionary Law would have granted workers and employees the right to share 30% of the profits of all the large industrial, mercantile and mining enterprises, including the sugar mills. The strictly agricultural enterprises would be exempt in consideration of other agrarian laws which would have been implemented.

The Fourth Revolutionary Law would have granted all planters the right to share 55% of the sugar production and a minimum quota of forty thousand "arrobas" (25 pounds) for all small planters who have been established for three or more years.

The Fifth Revolutionary Law would have ordered the confiscation of all holdings and ill-gotten gains of those who had committed frauds during previous regimes, as well as the holdings and ill-gotten gains of all their legatees and heirs. To implement this, special courts with full powers would gain access to all records of all corporations registered or operating in this country [in order] to investigate concealed funds of illegal origin, and to request that foreign governments extradite persons and attach holdings [rightfully belonging to the Cuban people]. Half of the property recovered would be used to subsidize retirement funds for workers and the other half would be used for hospitals, asylums and charitable organizations.

Furthermore, it was to be declared that the Cuban policy in the Americas would be one of close solidarity with the democratic people of this continent, and that those politically persecuted by bloody tyrants oppressing our sister nations would find generous asylum, brotherhood, and bread in the land of Marti. Not the persecution, hunger and treason that they find today. Cuba should be the bulwark of liberty and not a shameful link in the chain of despotism.

Eighty-five percent of the small farmers in Cuba pay rent and live under the constant threat of being dispossessed from the land that they cultivate. More than half the best cultivated land belongs to foreigners. In *Oriente*, the largest province, the lands of the United Fruit Company and West Indian Company join the north coast to the southern one. There are two hundred thousand peasant families who do not have a single acre of land to cultivate to provide food for their starving children. On the other hand, nearly three hundred thousand "caballerias" of productive land owned by powerful interests remains uncultivated.

Cuba is above all an agricultural state. Its population is largely rural. The city depends on these rural areas. The rural people won the Independence.

The greatness and prosperity of our country depends on a healthy and vigorous rural population that loves the land and knows how to cultivate it, with the framework of a state that protects and guides them. Considering all this, how can the present state of affairs be tolerated any longer?

The future of the country and the solution of its problems cannot continue to depend on the selfish interests of a dozen financiers, nor on the cold calculations of profits that ten or twelve magnates draw up in their air-conditioned offices. The country cannot continue begging on its knees for miracles from a few golden calves, similar to the Biblical one destroyed by the fury of a prophet. Golden calves cannot perform miracles of any kind. The problems of the Republic can be solved only if we dedicate ourselves to fight for that Republic with the same energy, honesty and patriotism our liberators had when they created it.

(Fidel Castro, *History Will Absolve Me*, foreword by Robert Taber (Lyle Stuart, 1961). Reprinted with permission of Kensington Publishing Company, pp. 35–38.)

THE ORDEAL OF HERBERT L. MATTHEWS

There was an answer to our desperate cries for help. Only one: yours.

—Mrs. María B. Amezaga, Matanzas, Cuba,
to Herbert L. Matthews, January 1959.

Clausewitz wrote of the fog of war; there is also a fog of history through which we journalists grope our way as best we can. At least we are in the midst of what is happening.

—Herbert L. Matthews, lecture, City College
of New York, March 15, 1961.

In the midst of this, Herbert L. Matthews retired from the *Times* in 1967 and lived in Australia until his death ten years later. Earlier Matthews had returned to the *Times* Editorial Board until his retirement. He published three major books and several pamphlets and articles defending his early coverage of Cuba and commenting upon the course of the Cuban Revolution after several more trips to the island. A newspaperman who worked for the *Times* for 45 years, he covered the Italian invasion of Abyssinia with an enthusiasm that later was to cause him pain, the Republican side during almost the whole course of the Spanish Civil War, the Allied invasion of Sicily and the entire Italian campaign. But it was his coverage of the Cuban Revolution that, toward the end of his career on the *Times*, was to cause him the most anguish of all. Although he walked out of his office on the tenth floor of the Times Building for the last time on September 10, 1967, carrying no grudges—perhaps some bitterness but not remorse—he had every reason to believe that he had done an honest job as a newspaperman and that his work would stand the test of time.

Matthews was aware that he would be judged harshly in the years immediately after the Cuban Revolution came to power on January 1, 1959. On March 31, 1961, eight months before Castro's "I am a Marxist-Leninist" speech, Matthews wrote in a memorandum to *Times* editors:

> My now famous criticism of the American press to the effect that in my nearly 40 years in journalism, I have never seen a big story so badly handled, is based on the fact that the American press has been very biased. This goes just as much for the pro-Fidel elements like Professor C. Wright Mills and the Fair Play for Cuba Committee as it does for the vast body of the American press which has been intensely hostile and emotional. . . . I believe I mentioned last year that it will take a long time for American public opinion to come around to a proper understanding of what happened in Cuba, at which time I have no doubt of the judgment on whatever I have written. As I recall I suggested this might take about 50 years, at which time I will be 110 years old.

Matthews was right in forecasting stormy times ahead. After repeated Cuban exile picket lines denounced him in front of the Times Building as late as 1964, after an alleged exile plot to kill him brought FBI protection, after receiving a massive volume of hate mail, after a bomb scare prevented him from concluding a speech at the University of New Mexico, after being dropped from the board of directors of the Inter American Press Association and almost being censured by that organization, and after being shunned at the Overseas Press Club, Matthews lived to savor a change in U.S. policy and—to a lesser extent—public opinion. He lived to witness Senator George McGovern's journey to Havana in 1975 as the first step toward including Cuba in the spirit of *détente*. Matthews also saw the groundwork being laid for an understanding of the rights over territorial waters between the two nations—and perhaps more importantly—the impetus toward reestablishing diplomatic relations by setting up information sections in both capitals. Matthews, who also lived to observe Cuban intervention in Africa, significantly subtitled his last work, *Revolution in Cuba* (1975), "An Essay in Understanding."

It is impossible in this brief paper to review in detail all of Matthews' work on Cuba. Some tentative evaluations are offered, but primarily this study is concerned with the impact of the original interview series in 1957 and subsequent articles through mid-1960, by which time the Marxist-Leninist alignment of Cuba was becoming clear. It examines the role of a journalist in the events he witnesses and reports. Can it or should it be one of complete detachment? Is he, as the New Journalism seems to say, an inevitable participant in the news process, and his participation should be honestly faced and his reactions honestly recorded? Herbert Matthews made his position clear quite early in this debate over objectivity in the journalism profession. In *The Education of a Correspondent*, published in 1946, he declared:

> True journalism, like true historiography, is not mere chronology, not (to cite Von Ranke's famous definition of the purpose of history) "simply to describe the event exactly as it happened," but placing the event in its proper category *as a moral act and judging it as such.*

Again, in *The Yoke and the Arrows*, a book-length account of Franco's Spain published in 1961, Matthews stated quite candidly:

> I would never dream of hiding my own bias or denying it. I did not do so during the Spanish Civil War and I do not do so now. In my credo, as I said before, the journalist is not one who must be free of bias or opinions or feelings. Such a newspaperman would be a pitiful specimen, to be despised rather than admired. There is only one test that means anything, only one quality that the reader has a right to demand—the truth as the man sees it and all the truth. He must never change or suppress that truth; he must never present as the truth anything that he does not honestly believe to be true.

What truth did Matthews find in the Sierra Maestra in 1957? In the first place, he was no Stanley looking for a Dr. Livingstone: that is, he was not engaged in a journalistic lark or performing a journalistic stunt. Since 1949, Matthews had been a member of the Editorial Board of the New York *Times* specializing in Latin American affairs. In 1952 he covered the opening phase of the Bolivian National Revolution with such empathy that he was decorated by the Bolivian revolutionary government in 1959. The *Times* printed his editorials opposing such dictators—in the decade which Tad Szulc of the *Times* prematurely called *Twilight of the Tyrants*—as Juan Domingo Perón of Argentina, overthrow in 1955; Anastasio Somozo of Nicaragua, 1956; Gustavo Rojas Piñilla of Colombia, 1957, and Marcos Pérez Jiménez of Venezuela, 1958.

Thus, Matthews had wide-ranging knowledge of Latin American realities, but it was only after Castro's re-entry into Cuba with the 82-man *Granma* expedition on December 2, 1956, that Matthews became keenly interested in the fate of Fulgencio Batista, who had dominated Cuban politics for a quarter of a century, either behind the scenes or after grabbing power before the scheduled elections of 1952. Francis L. McCarthy, head of the United Press bureau in Havana, reported that Castro had been killed in the *Granma* landing, and a few days later sent another dispatch describing the place where he was buried. Over the protests of Mrs. Ruby Hart Phillips, the *Times'* resident correspondent in Cuba, the *Times* front-paged the original UP story of Castro's death. As Mrs. Phillips recalled later, "Apparently, McCarthy's information came from an officer in the Cuban air force, who had taken part in the air attack on the Castro expedition and who was enthusiastic about the accuracy of his bombing."

Actually, only a handful of men, including Fidel, Raúl Castro and Ernesto Ché Guevara, had made it into the Sierra Maestra, but no one in the outside world and only a few Cubans knew this until the first of a three-part series of Matthews' interview with Castro appeared on the front page of the *Times* on February 24, 1957. That is, for almost three months there was total silence from Fidel, a remarkable achievement in itself. With typical bravado, he had radioed ahead from Mexico his invasion plans, hoping to arouse popular support, but also signalling Batista authorities to be on the watch for him. Fidel Castro was not a major figure in the world press at that time. He was a troublesome nuisance whom Batista believed to be dead and some Cubans feared was dead. The incident seemed to be closed, in the view of many, with one more idealistic and hot-headed young Cuban rebel cut down at the age of 29. It was all part of the passing scene.

Then a remarkable thing happened, which demonstrates the enormous power of the New York *Times*—when it chooses to use it—and why the Western press calls itself the Fourth Estate. Matthews scored the Latin American journalistic *coup* of the century in resurrecting Fidel Castro. Not exactly modest, the *Times* correspondent devoted about half of his first installment to the dangers involved in getting into and out of the Sierra Maestra, which was ringed with Batista's troops. Matthews later published a fuller account of how he got the scoop. But, since the Matthews Papers have become available at the Colombia University Library, these have been relied upon to piece together this account, adding details not previously published. Original sources from almost everyone concerned are available, for Matthews later asked the participants to write their firsthand accounts. That was done after former U.S. Ambassador to Cuba Arthur Gardner, an admirer and friend of Batista, apparently had testified falsely before the Senate Internal Security Subcommittee on August 27, 1960, that he had arranged the trip into the Sierra Maestra on condition that Matthews would share any information gleaned with the U.S. Embassy staff in Havana.

What actually happened? As Mrs. Phillips, who had been covering Cuban affairs for the *Times* since 1931, reconstructed events, René Rodríguez—one of the survivors of the *Granma* landing—came to Havana from the Sierra

Maestra in late January, 1957. His mission was to inform Faustino Pérez, acting chief of the 26th of July Movement in the capital, that Castro wanted to be interviewed by a foreign correspondent to prove he was still alive. Javier Pazos, a Havana University student active in the movement, was designated to make the arrangements. He conferred with his father Felipe Pazos, former head of the National Bank of Cuba and another active supporter of Castro's cause. As Javier explained later, "In part, the reason for wanting a foreign correspondent was due to Batista's press censorship, but it also reflected the resentment and general dislike that we all shared towards the almost totally corrupt national press." The only foreign correspondent that the elder Pazos knew was Ruby Hart Phillips, and so he turned to her. His account of what followed, although laced with Cuban humor, reveals the atmosphere of fear that pervaded Batista's Cuba:

> I phoned Ruby Phillips . . . and asked her to receive me. So she did in her house-office, where there were three or four more people and a relatively heavy traffic of persons entering and leaving—boys from the grocery and the drugstore, maids, friends, etc. At my request for a private talk, she took me to an adjoining room without any door to separate it from the hall, where the other people were, five yards apart at most. I told her in a whisper that Fidel Castro wanted a foreign correspondent to visit him at the Sierra and she answered in a loud and most penetrating voice, that could be heard one block away—"So, you have contact with Fidel Castro! I cannot believe it! Please, tell me all you know." I cannot recall any occasion in my whole life, neither before nor afterwards, when I had a [so] ardent desire to kill someone.

Mrs. Phillips, incredulous, insisted on talking with René Rodríguez, the Castro emissary, herself. Pazos recalled, "At this point I should have ended the conversation and started to look for some other correspondent, but it was not prudent to quarrell [sic] with Mrs. Phillips at this stage and so I promised her to arrange a meeting with the man from the mountains." The meeting took place one or two days later in Pazos' office in the Bacardí Building. On that occasion, he remembered, "Ruby asked everything on heaven and earth (this time in a very low voice of conspirational [sic] tones, in spite that all doors and windows were closed and the room sound conditioned). . . ."

Mrs. Phillips recalled, "They told me frankly a woman would be too conspicious [sic], especially an American, and asked if I could send someone. . . . As I walked back to [my] office a few blocks away I met Ted Scott of NBC. He came back with me and I told him the whole story since we were good friends and I trusted him. . . . I asked Ted if he were interested and he said no for the same reason I had, that he would have to leave Cuba. Then Ted suggested that we get you [Matthews] to do [it]."

Edward W. Scott, the NBC reporter who also wrote a column for the Havana *Post*, picks up the story:

> In my presence, Ruby sat down at the typewriter and wired Emmanuel Freedman, Foreign Editor of the New York *Times*, suggesting that you should come to Havana immediately. She showed me the cable and I felt that it was properly worded. Of course, it did not make any suggestion as to the reason why Ruby wanted you to come to Havana.

Within a few days Matthews and his wife Nancie arrived in Havana; he had planned a Cuban trip anyway to check out persistent rumors that Castro was alive. After an interview with the elder Pazos, a party of five set out in a jeep for Manzanillo, the jumping-off place in Oriente Province. They included Matthews and his wife, posing as middle-aged American tourists or, if they were caught with the money the others were taking to Castro, as a businessman and his wife interested in buying land in the easternmost province of Cuba where the Sierra Maestra is located. They were accompanied by Faustino Pérez, hunted by the police because he headed the July 26th Movement in Havana, known to Matthews only as "Luis," and Liliam Mesa, known only as "Marta," to protect their identities, and Javier Pazos, who was peeved at the presence of Liliam Mesa, a Havana society girl, because, as he wrote later to Matthews, "I didn't want you to take the impression that it was a country fair. . . ."

After driving the 600-mile length of the island overnight, Matthews got a few hours rest at the home of Manzanillo schoolteachers Pedro and Ena Saumell, where Mrs. Matthews was to stay overnight while the rendezvous with Castro took place. The dangers and doubts of the arduous journey, partly by jeep and then on foot, into the Sierra Maestra for the actual interview with Castro need not be recounted here. With the flair of a Richard Harding Davis, Matthews provided the exciting details that took up almost one-half of the first installment on February 24, 1957, which occupied almost a full page of the *Times* after the story was continued from the front page. On the way back to New York, the seven small pages of Matthews' notes, bearing Castro's signature to authenticate them, had gone through Cuban customs tucked inside Mrs. Matthews' girdle. The newspaperman began writing his story aboard the plane, but the first installment was held up for a week so it could be promoted for the Sunday edition of February 24, 1957.

When the interview with Castro did appear in print, it was by any standards a journalistic bombshell. As with any human enterprise, it contained errors—some later acknowledged by Matthews and others not. The best-known miscalculation was the size of the rebel band in the Sierra Maestra: Castro told Matthews that Batista had 3,000 men in the field against them, deployed in columns of 200, against "[us] in groups of ten to forty." There was another reference to 50 telescopic rifles which the insurgents had, whereas—as Fidel later boasted at the Overseas Press Club when he visited the United States in April, 1959—at the time of the Matthews interview Castro had only 18 armed men.

In the original story, Matthews also stated, "The reports reaching Havana that frequent clashes were taking place and that the Government troops were losing heavily proved true." This was clearly an exaggeration at that time. Matthews also erred in reporting that the Cuban Communist Party, *Partido Socialista Popular* (PSP), "naturally bolsters all the opposition (to Batista) elements." This was not true. The PSP had dismissed Castro as a petty bourgeois reformer—a judgment based upon his "History Will Absolve Me" speech of 1953—and later refused to heed his call for a general strike on April 8, 1958, perhaps fearing by that time he would steal their thunder.

What about Castro himself? Noting his "extraordinary eloquence," Matthews wrote:

> The personality of the man is overpowering. It was easy to see why he has caught the imagination of the youth of Cuba all over the island. Here was an educated, dedicated fanatic, a man of ideals, of courage and of remarkable qualities of leadership. . . . [O]ne got a feeling that he is now invincible. Perhaps he isn't, but that is the faith he inspires in his followers.

Those who maintain that the *Times* "created" Castro should consult the installment of February 25 in which Matthews wrote, "The dictator [Batista] has lost the young generation of Cuba. The group of young rebels, led by former law student Fidel Castro, that dominates the Sierra Maestra at the eastern end of the island and that is fighting off successfully the cream of General Batista's army *is only one element*—the most dramatic one—to prove this" (stress added). And in the final installment of February 26, Matthews wrote that the directorate of the Federation of University Students "are fighting a parallel, separate fight for the same goals." He concluded the series with this paragraph:

> So one sees three elements lining up against President Batista today—the youth of Cuba, led by the fighting rebel, Fidel Castro, who are against the President to a man, a civic resistance formed of respected political, business and professional groups, and an honest patriotic component of the Army, which is ashamed of the actions of the Government generals. Together these elements form the hope of Cuba and the threat to General Fulgencio Batista.

It was, however, the first story of February 24, 1957, which caused a splash so big it amazed Matthews himself. There was such a demand for that Sunday edition of the *Times* among Batista exiles in Miami that copies were black-marketed for $1.50 each. According to Robert Taber, a CBS documentary maker, "Before the day was out, the Cuban underground [in Miami] was busily producing photostatic copies for distribution in Cuba, and was working on a translation." Since censorship of incoming as well as outgoing news was in effect in Cuba, Matthews' stories were literally cut out of the February 24 and 25 editions which reached Havana. The effort seemed useless, however, as Raoul Alfonso Gonsé, director of *El Mundo* of Havana, wrote Matthews on February 25 that his story "has been a sensation in Cuba." Gonsé noted that he had received a summary of the last installment by cable "and moreover, I have obtained a smuggled copy of it."

Perhaps because Batista officials believed the story to be a fake and hoped to discredit the *Times*, censorship was lifted before the end of the state of siege and the February 26 edition arrived intact. As Richard G. Cushing, an official of the United States Information Service in Havana and a news source for Matthews, wrote on February 26, "Now that the censorship is off (as of today) reproduction of the articles is a certainty in the local press." To Ted Scott of NBC, Cushing wrote, "Herb Matthews may qualify for the Pulitzer Prize for his Castro scoop. I understand the Cuban government is issuing a flat denial . . .—an odd procedure considering the prestige of the paper and of the writer."

The interview was vigorously denounced by Edmund Chester, a former CBS executive who worked as public relations counselor for the Batista regime. Believing that Castro was dead and the story a fake, Chester issued a stout denial through Santiago Verdeja, Minister of National Defense, calling the story "a chapter in a fantastic novel." The *Times* published the text of this denial on February 28, along with a reply by Matthews and a photograph (retouched because of the poor light) showing him interviewing Castro.

Meanwhile, Batista refugees staged a demonstration in support of Matthews in front of the *Times* building, and messages of congratulations poured into his office. As Matthews wrote to Turner Catledge, the *Times'* chief news executive, "I never in my thirty-five years on the Times have received such a flood of letters and telegrams as I have had this time." Ted Scott of NBC News called Matthews' account of the interview "the summit story of an exciting career." Scott also joked, "For the nonce [Feb. 28, 1957], your aristocratic name is a stench in official nostrils at the 23rd Parallel, but the Opposition is proposing constitutional reforms so that you can be elected President." Edward W. Barrett, dean of the Columbia University Graduate School of Journalism, noted, "It was wonderful to see the old firehorse in operation again." And Alberto Gainza Paz, owner of *La Prensa* of Buenos Aires, called Matthews' journalistic feat "the outstanding story of the year."

Matthews perhaps winced—or smiled—at some of the praise, such as that by John A. Brogan, Jr., of King Features Syndicate, who wrote that the scoop "reminds me of the good old Hearstian accomplishments." Brogan also referred to Matthews' "catastrophic achievement" when he apparently meant "cataclysmic." And in an inter-office memorandum, Harrison E. Salisbury called Matthews' attention to "a small and rather grudging bouquet" that had appeared in Moscow's *Literary Gazette*. In a one-third column report headed, "Useful Trip," the Soviet publication falsely charged that Matthews had been writing editorials in New York supporting American puppets such as Batista. The story continued:

[Then] Matthews left his writing desk and went on a trip to Cuba. Matthews travelled all over the country and even went to the mountains of the Sierra Madre [sic] where a group of rebels headed by the former student Fidelio [sic] is active. Matthews wrote about the bitter terror saddled on Cuba by Dictator Batista.

If any Cuban official still doubted the authenticity of Matthews' story, the doubts were laid to rest when Robert Taber and Wendell Hoffman of CBS made their way into the Sierra Maestra in April to do a documentary shown on U.S. television on May 19, 1957. *Bohemia*, the popular Cuban weekly review, stated:

The film documentary of the Columbia Broadcasting System terminated a chapter in the record of developments in the Sierra Maestra. After that sensational report, lively testimony to the rebel presence in the mountains, it was known for certain that hostilities would break [out], putting an end to long weeks of doubt and rumors.

Matthews returned to Cuba to interview Batista on June 5, 1957. There he was allowed to submit only written questions to the Cuban dictator. In a reply, probably drafted by Chester, Batista dismissed Castro as a criminal and reproached the *Times* correspondent:

There is [now] no censorship in Cuba, Mr. Matthews, and you know very well that my government has never interfered with you in your work as a journalist in Cuba—even though you associated with known criminals and pleaded the cause of a man who has taken up arms in an effort to overthrow the constituted government. You have always had at least as much freedom in Cuba as you have had in your own country, despite the fact that you have consistently written stories that were unfavorable to my person, my government and to the Cuban people.

Batista officials also counter-attacked in another way against what they considered to be a concerted effort by Matthews to bring down the Cuban regime. On June 18, 1957, Cuba made an official protest to the Council of the Organization of American States (OAS) regarding statements Matthews had made on a CBS panel interview the previous Sunday. As the newsman reported to his boss, Emmanuel Freedman, foreign editor of the *Times*, "The protest was referred to a meeting of the entire 13-member General Committee of the OAS last evening where the sentiment against Cuba was so overwhelming that the Cuban Ambassador, in order to avoid a humiliating defeat, was permitted to withdraw his complaint."

On August 11, 1957, Matthews published an article, "The Shadow Falls on Cuba's Batista," in *The New York Times Magazine*. By now the journalist was stepping up the timetable for the collapse of the Batista regime. The second paragraph of this article stated:

> . . . the long reign of Fulgencio Batista is coming to an end. The writing on the Cuban wall, however cryptic as to the exact time and manner of departure, is clear enough. Even granting his own wish to finish out this term of office, Batista would retire on Feb. 1, 1959, a year and a half from now. Few Cubans today would give him that long a lease on power.

The article, detailing brutality and corruption in Batista's regime of recent years, also presented the positive aspects of the man's long career. Castro was mentioned only in reference to the "well-trained, desperate, enthusiastic young rebels under Fidel Castro in the Sierra Maestra of Oriente Province." The article concluded:

> It took character, courage, political mastery, administrative ability and popular appeal [for Batista] to reach the heights and stay there for twenty-four years. But now there is a sense of implacable history closing in on Fulgencio Batista. He is a man at bay, fighting a rearguard action, bravely and effectively. But for how long?

As in the closing paragraph of the original series of three articles, this statement could be considered a call for action by Batista's opponents to close in for the kill: he was wounded and limping badly. At any rate, Batista's opponents made the most of Matthews' article. René Zayas Bazán of the Cuban underground movement mailed Matthews a mimeographed copy of his article translated into Spanish and noted that "it is being passed from hand to hand among the [Cuban] population."

The *Times'* coverage of Castro's guerrilla warfare began to diverge between conflicting reports by Mrs. Phillips, resident correspondent in Havana, and Matthews, who had his own news sources whose letters were smuggled out of Cuba. The break between the latter and Mrs. Phillips began to appear behind the scenes when Matthews complained in a memorandum to Freedman, foreign editor of the *Times*, on June 19, 1957, "Incidentally, about four weeks ago Ruby had the Govt launching the most terrific en[d]-all, mop-up campaign against Fidel ever. Now what? From my information Fidel is going just as strong as ever. Shouldn't we have a follow up?"

Indeed, in many instances Matthews had better long-distance news sources than Mrs. Phillips had on the scene. For example, he received a five-page, single-spaced letter from Juan Marinello, leader of the PSP, the Cuban Communist party, who explained on March 17, 1957:

> . . . we consider that this [July 26] Group encourages noble aims but, in general, proceeds with wrong tactics. Therefore we do not agree with its actions, but we call upon all the parties and popular sectors to defend it against the blows of the tyranny, not forgetting that those who make up that Movement are fighting a government abhorred by all the Cuban people.

Raúl Chibás, a Castro supporter who had been president of the Ortodoxo party in the 1950s, kept Matthews informed of the Movimiento de Resistencia Cívica, which Chibás asserted in a letter of April 16, 1957, had spread from Oriente to the other five provinces. Mario Llerena, who was to be in charge of Propaganda and Public Relations after Castro established a July 26 Committee in exile in the United States on October 30, 1957, reported to Matthews from Havana on May 12, 1957: "I am confident about our ultimate victory. I feel sure about it. Fidel gains stature and prestige day by day. Our men have a solid and unbreakable morale."

Some of the information Matthews received was fairly accurate and other reports grossly exaggerated. In the former category, Armando Hart, who was to become Minister of Education after Castro gained power, wrote on November 4, 1957, that the number of men and arms had increased five-fold in the eight months since Matthews' interview with Castro. But in the latter category were such overblown statements as that of July 6, 1958, by Rufo López-Fresquet, who was to serve as Minister of the Treasury before fleeing Castro's Cuba, that "Rebel forces have grown to 20,000 in Oriente, close to 1,000 in Cubitas Hills, Camagüey, and over 2,000 in the Trinidad Mountains."

Nevertheless, the momentum of the rebellion increased until Batista and others of his entourage fled to the Dominican Republic on January 1, 1959. They left behind a well equipped and well trained Army of some 40,000 men demoralized and defeated by the corruption and brutality of their own officers by an original band of about a score of men who caught the imagination of an outraged populace. When Castro made his triumphal week-long tour the length of the island, from Santiago to Havana, Matthews was there to witness it with a rebel press pass with a notation typed in capital letters, EDITORI-ALISTA ESPECIAL. Turner Catledge, chief news executive for the *Times*, wrote from New York:

> You've done just what I predicted in my cable of congratulations of January 2—"Kept us ahead of the pack." We are grateful and through this note want you to know it. Many, many thanks. I know you and Nancy [sic] have enjoyed being in the thick of it. But take care of yourselves. Warmest regards.

Castro was a hero throughout the United States, but the warm regards were not to last long. First to alienate the U.S. press were the summary trials and executions of *batistiano* "war criminals" in January, 1959. But, as Matthews noted later in an article for the British publication *Encounter*:

> Virtually all Cubans approved or accepted the executions as necessary, but for an American to express understanding and to make the point that the trials and executions, however contrary to the normal traditions of Anglo-Saxon legality, were rough justice and a sensible method of preventing mob violence and private vengeance was considered outrageous.

By the time Castro made his visit to the United States in April 1959, as historian Hubert Herring has pointed out, "The American press had angered Fidel by its denunciation of his highhanded ways . . . [and in return] was accused of being subsidized by pro-Batista elements."

Matthews was alarmed at the reportage in the *Times* itself. He wrote to Arthur Hays Sulzberger, chairman of the board, on July 18, 1959, "Ruby Phillips has been very emotional and very hostile and she, too, despite her experience, is essentially an amateur." Matthews asked for and obtained permission to go to Cuba himself for a week or ten days. Mrs. Phillips recalled later that after he arrived Matthews "was irritated because I did not exhibit any enthusiasm for the Castro revolution." In his story, Matthews referred to Fidel as "the young man who single-handled has made the history of Cuba today." He added"

> Half a year after the revolt against the Batista regime, Cuba is in the midst of the first great social revolution in Latin America since the Mexican Revolution of 1910. This is not a Communist revolution in any sense of the word and there are no Communists in positions of control. . . .There seem to be very few [persons] in Cuba—and one need have no hesitation in saying this—who believe Fidel Castro is a Communist, is under Communist influence or is a dupe of communism. . . .

Mrs. Phillips recalled later in her book, "The Cuban Dilemma" (1962), "It hardly seemed possible to me that the Cubans could be so blind and Herbert so stubborn in his refusal to see."

Matthews was correct, however, at the time he was writing in mid-1959, with two exceptions. He overlooked the significance of the Bolivian National Revolution which got underway in 1952, and he did not realize that Raúl Castro and Che Guevara were both Marxists of long standing, an error carried over into his book *The Cuban Story* (1961). Perhaps Matthews was so adamant on the point of communism in July, 1959, because on the previous day the *Times* had front-paged the testimony before a Senate subcommittee of Major Pedro Díaz Lanz, former head of the Cuban Air Force who had fled Cuba on June 29. He charged, in the words of the reporter covering the story, that "Premier Fidel Castro was the chief Communist in Cuba and a member of the international Communist conspiracy."

Time magazine took advantage of the divergent views of Matthews and Mrs. Phillips to attack the former in its edition of July 27, 1959, contrasting their coverage of the rapidly unfolding Cuban story. The article also lifted quotations out of context from Matthews' *The Education of a Correspondent* (1946) to castigate him for noting "the charm and hospitality of the Japanese" in 1929, and for supporting Mussolini's invasion of Ethiopia in 1935. His coverage of the Republicans during the Spanish Civil War also came under attack, and the piece concluded that in Cuba, Matthews is "viewed more as a revolutionary institution than a working newsman."

William Attwood, foreign editor of *Look*, fired off a letter to John Koffend, editor of the Press section of *Time*:

[I want you to] know how shocked I was to read the piece about Herbert Matthews. I have seen many examples of non-journalism in TIME over the years, but this is the first one I've noticed in which a newspaperman is singled out by a publication for professional demolition. You don't have to agree with Matthews' views to be dismayed by such editorial arrogance—especially in a magazine that makes a point of deploring McCarthyism.

Matthews ignored such personal attacks, but he was profoundly alarmed and concerned about what most of the U.S. press was doing, consciously and unconsciously, in its coverage of the Cuban Revolution. He fought valiantly to keep the Communist label from being slapped on Fidel, believing this attitude was pushing the Cuban leader into a corner. As Matthews wrote to Philip W. Bonsal, U.S. ambassador to Cuba, on July 27, 1959:

I feel most of all that the attacks on Cuba and on Fidel Castro and his associates for being Communist or pro-Communist, are achieving exactly the opposite effect from what we all want. Senators Eastland, Keating, Dodd and company, are God's gift to the Cuban Communists. So are *Time* and *Life* magazines and many other columnists and commentators who so stupidly attack the Castro regime without a proper basis for such attacks. In so doing they make it just about impossible for Fidel to take an openly anti-Communist line.

By early 1960, Matthews was coming under attack from many quarters. When the *Saturday Evening Post* ran an editorial calling Castro a "crackpot surrounded by Communist operators," the Rev. Ira E. Sherman of a Methodist church in Matanzas province sent the editor a copy of a paper presented by Matthews at Stanford University. Frederick Nelson, senior editor of the *Post*, replied, "Herbert Matthews of the New York Times seems to have been the father of the Castro movement, as he was of the abortive movement in Spain twenty-odd years ago." In sending a copy of the reply to Matthews, the Rev. Sherman commented, "I thought you would be surprised to learn that you are considered to be the father of the Spanish Republic."

But it was within the *Times* itself that Matthews was to be tested most severely. James Reston, head of the *Times* Washington bureau, wrote a news analysis on Cuba, which appeared on February 19, 1960, and which began, "Cuba's drift to the Left is causing more concern here than any event in the hemisphere since the Communist threat to Guatemala in 1954." Reston was disturbed by the visit to Cuba of Anastas I. Mikoyan, one of the two First Deputy Premiers of the Soviet Union, and asked, "What, for example, if the Soviet Union negotiated a mutual security pact with Cuba . . .? Could Washington tolerate such a move? Could it prevent such a move without landing the Marines in Cuba?"

On the same day that Reston's column appeared, Matthews wrote an earnest letter to his friend:

> You write as if it were possible for Cuba to be another Guatemala and for the situation to be handled quite simply as in the past by sending Marines. . . .Another feature of this situation that I think should be called to your attention is that Guatemala became so dangerous more than anything because of our inept and very misguided diplomacy. . . . If certain pressures force us into taking strong measures against Cuba I think that almost anything can happen, and whatever it is would be very bad for the United States as well as Cuba and Latin America.

Reston replied: "So long as this remains merely as a revolutionary situation nobody with even the vaguest knowledge of that country [Cuba] in the past can be anything but sympathetic. But once there is a drift toward conspiracy linked to Moscow then it is a whole new ball game."

The upshot of this exchange was that Reston went to Cuba himself and wrote a couple of stories which agreed with Mrs. Phillips, much to her delight, that Cuba was indeed moving toward a Communist form of government. In the infighting at the *Times*, Matthews had lost and his ordeal was about to begin.

Between August, 1960, and August, 1964, he faced attack from the Senate Internal Security Subcommittee. Matthews recalled in his memoir, "At each of the ten or more hearings my name and supposed misdemeanors figured more or less prominently." Nevertheless, he was not called as a witness and given the chance to defend himself. More seriously, the hearings wrecked the careers of Roy R. Rubottom, Jr., the Assistant Secretary of State, and William A. Wieland, head of the Caribbean desk of the Bureau of Inter-American Affairs.

It was ironic to link Matthews with these two men, because he differed with them on Department of State policy, and on at least one occasion he tried to act directly as intermediary between the United States and Cuba. On July 21, 1960, Matthews had lunch with Raúl Roa, Cuban foreign minister, and other Cuban officials at the United Nations. Then the newspaperman wrote Rubottom, "They wanted me to note the fact that although they are accused of being a satellite of the Soviet Union he carefully abstained from seeing any of the Russians at any time" during his visit to New York. Matthews added:

> Their insistence all along was on their acknowledged dependence on the Soviet block economically but that they had no commitment of any sort politically. The visit of Raúl Castro to Moscow, I gather, was simply a defiant gesture toward the United States. They insisted that he had no intention on this trip of negotiating for arms.

Matthews concluded that it was not his custom to pass along to third parties information that he received personally and confidentially, but that he was doing so in this instance because he had the "decided impression" that Roa and the others wanted him to do so.

Although Matthews received a long, official reply from Rubottom, the State Department official expressed himself more frankly in a handwritten note:

> In all honesty, I doubt that Roa could negotiate with the U.S. even if he wanted to, which is open to doubt. They had countless opportunities before positions got where they are today, but never seized a one.

Matthews answered, "I feel that we have not left Fidel Castro any real opening if or when the time comes that he would like to try to reach an understanding with us."

By late 1960 and early 1961, Matthews was receiving a flood of hate mail, and the pickets outside the *Times* building by then were hostile. He wrote

Arthur Hays Sulzberger on February 2, 1961, only two months before the Bay of Pigs invasion:

> These letters about Cuba prove to me once again what I have been arguing all along—that a dangerous emotionalism has developed in the United States over the situation. It is dangerous because it affects Congress and that in turn brings pressure on the State Department.

Matthews found himself increasingly isolated on the *Times* staff itself. For example, Francis Brown, editor of the *New York Times Book Review*, refused to use Matthews' review of C. Wright Mills' *Listen Yankee-The Revolution in Cuba* (1960). The *Times* correspondent Tad Szulc did the review, even though he was not in Cuba when Mills, a professor of sociology at Columbia University, made his observations, whereas Matthews was. His rejected review began:

> The academic world has been waking up to the true significance of the Cuban revolution before our mass communications media. This was perhaps to be expected because there is a goodly number of Latin Americanists in our universities and very few in journalism.

The pressure was on Matthews from the management of the *Times* as well. As he described the showdown in his memoir:

> The atmosphere was getting so hot for *The Times* that late in the summer of 1961, Orvil Dryfoos, then president and publisher, called me to his office. He was cordial and pleasant, but also upset and worried. The gist of what he said was that somehow a truce must be called in the battle between me and my critics, as it was proving too embarrassing to *The Times*. . . .The main result of our talk was that I did not try to visit Cuba again for two and a half years, thereby losing touch—which was bad for *The Times* as well as for me, and I also cut down on my lecturing.

For solace, Matthews wrote to his friend and fellow war correspondent Ernest Hemingway, stating simply, "I feel more than ever a need for moral support." Matthews mentioned the book by the ex-Marxist Nathaniel Weyl, *Red Star Over Cuba* (1961), and commented sardonically, "It should have been called 'Red Star Over Times Square' since it is mostly about me." Matthews explained in his letter to Hemingway:

> I try to keep out of all controversies on Cuba and never answer attacks. The only reason I called [Ambassador Arthur] Gardner a perjurer was that he tried to besmirch a reputation I have spent nearly 40 years in building of never faking stories and also because it seemed important to keep the historic record straight.

Later, Matthews was to date the beginning of the rapprochement between Castro and the Cuban Communists as about mid-1960. On May 25 of that year Matthews received a letter from his trusted friend Helen López-Fresquet in Cuba, who informed him, "I can't rationalize any longer. This country is being run completely by the communists, and it looks more and more as though that is just the way Fidel planned it and wants to continue it." Matthews did not agree on the last point because he believed that Castro had been sincere and honest in whatever he said at any given moment in a rapidly unfolding social revolution. As Matthews had written to Carlos Todd of the *Times of Havana* on March 16, 1959, "I find it impossible to believe that anyone who has felt the way he [Castro] did and fought for seven years, can change overnight."

No one has proved otherwise. Yet as Matthews recalled later, "for forty-eight hours after Fidel made his famous `I am a Marxist-Leninist' speech on December 1–2, 1961, I went through the worst period of my career." The UPI reported that Fidel had declared in the speech that he had been a Communist since his student days. But when the full official text became available, it was clear, as Matthews put it, that "he was apologizing for *not* having been one and for being so slow in approaching the virtues of Marxism."

In conclusion, did Fidel Castro get his job through the New York *Times*, as a caricature in the *National Review* depicted him as saying? The overwhelming weight of evidence indicates that such an exaggeration was amusing but unjustified. On the face of it, it is witless to suggest that Matthews of the New York *Times* invented created Fidel Castro. This, as the *Hispanic American Report* once said, "is as absurd as blaming a meteorologist for a thunderstorm." Or as Matthews himself expressed it in his 1969 biography of Castro, "No amount of sensational publicity would have meant anything in the course of a short time if Fidel Castro had not been just as I described him." Both the Senate Internal Security Subcommittee and the public at large sought to place blame for "losing" Cuba to communism, and Matthews was a prime target. The Senate body declared that Matthews had made Castro "a Robin Hood of the Sierra Maestra," and even the distinguished British historian Hugh Thomas wrote that Matthews and later the CBS documentary team "created . . . a hero, a legend, a T.E. Lawrence of the Caribbean."

Such exaggerations should not obscure the fact that the Matthews interview did have considerable impact throughout the hemisphere. Some observers believed it gave Castro a decisive boost on his road to power. Edward W. Scott, the NBC representative in Havana, for example, wrote to Matthews in 1961, "I have said in the press and I reiterate that I think your trip to the Sierra to interview Fidel saved the Castro revolution from utter defeat and paved the way for its success." And José M. Bosch, president of the Bacardí Company and one who opposed both Batista and Castro, also wrote to Matthews in 1961, "To Fidel you are the equivalent of an army division, so winning you away will be quite a victory!"

As for the conflict within the *Times* itself, Matthews has made it clear that it was for him a family quarrel or argument. As he wrote in a letter of January 20, 1976, the *Times* "had to absorb a great deal of criticism for my work, and let it run longer than any other paper would have, since they trusted my ability and integrity." Nevertheless, Matthews was returned to his editorial-writing position, and the *Times* did not use news articles offered by him after trips to Cuba in 1963 and 1966. On the latter occasion, he was gathering material for his biography of Castro, and after his retirement in 1967 he went to the island one more time in 1972 to collect data for his book *Revolution in Cuba, An Essay in Understanding* (1975). Thus, on two occasions the *Times* missed the opportunity to present to its readers unique views of what was happening inside revolutionary Cuba. Turner Catledge, then chief news executive of the *Times*, presented his side of the story in his memoir published in 1971:

> On at least two occasions we declined to publish articles by Matthews on Cuba. . . . To put it simply, I felt that Matthews, despite certain obvious changes in judgment, had lost his credibility as a reporter on Castro, and that to print his articles would do the *Times* more harm than good. I reached the decision with reluctance, but I thought it was necessary to protect the *Times'* credibility.

Catledge said the *Times* had worked hard to earn its high reputation "for responsible reporting and reasoned editorializing."

Part of Matthews' difficulty may have been that much of the U.S. press— and therefore the U.S. public—was poorly educated in Latin American affairs. Matthews wrote in 1976:

> The problem is one of *sustained* interest. When there is a revolution or assassination, of course, some news is printed. I decided that it was a vicious circle: readers are generally interested in what is familiar to them; since they are *not* interested in Latin America, editors will not provide money, personnel or space to educate them.

Matthews also felt that readers were predisposed to believe the most unfavorable reports about Latin America. His analysis of why most of the U.S. press had bungled the Cuban story:

> Readers or radio and television listeners believed (in fact, wanted to believe) the worst about Cuba long before it became as bad as they thought. The result of this type of approach was to bring about, or to hasten, this "worst," and that is

what can happen whenever a leftist revolutionary situation develops or threatens in Latin America or anywhere else in the world.

In other words, he continued, "The American mass media . . . tend to create a fantastic world. The picture they draw is a response to a predisposed public opinion which is both satisfied and molded by it."

Moral courage in reporting the truth as one sees it is not to be condemned, and coverage of the Cuban Revolution by Matthews will stand the test of time. He reported a Cuban response to a Cuban crisis during the Cold War, and for telling the truth as he saw it he was vilified: the messenger was confused with the message. As Eduardo Santos, publisher of *El Tiempo* of Bogotá and former president of Colombia (1938–1942), wrote to Matthews in 1960 about his coverage of the Cuban Revolution:

> There are seductive aspects which you point out beautifully. There are others less attractive and some detestable. But as you say one is dealing with a *Revolution*, and Revolutions never have been pretty, nor peaceful, nor totally prudent and just. But they are almost always-alas!-necessary.

(Jerry W. Knudson, "Herbert L. Matthews and the Cuban Story," *Journalism Monographs*, No. 54 (February 1978), 1–22.)

Hacienda of San Juan de Chinameca where Emiliano Zapata was assassinated on April 11, 1919. Such fortress-like buildings guarded the patron's vast holdings before the Revolution. Photos by Jerry W. Knudson, except as noted.

Mateo Zapata, one of five children of the agrarian reform leader, Cuautla, 1961. Today, he objects to the use of his father's name by the Zapatista National Liberation Army in the dormant Chiapas uprising which began in 1994.

The face of Mexico. Policarpo Castro, one of two surviving Zapatistas in the village of Anenecuilco, where Emiliano Zapata was born. He fought with him. This photo was taken in 1961 when he was revered by the villagers.

The face of Mexico. Ricarda Ayonn, one of two surviving Zapatistas in the village of Anenecuilco, where Emiliano Zapata was born. She fought with him. This photo was taken in 1961 when she was revered by the villagers.

Rene Barrientos, who in 1964 overthrew President Victor Paz Estenssoro, chief architect of the Movimiento Nacionalista Revoluciario (MNR) which began transformation of Bolivia after 1952. Barrientos was elected President in 1996 and came down hard on the tin miners.

Che Guevara, posing as a middle-aged businessman, entered Bolivia in 1967 undetected at the El Alto airport. This photo, taken at the base camp in the rugged terrain and rain forest of southeast Bolivia, was published after his death. Courtesy of El Diario.

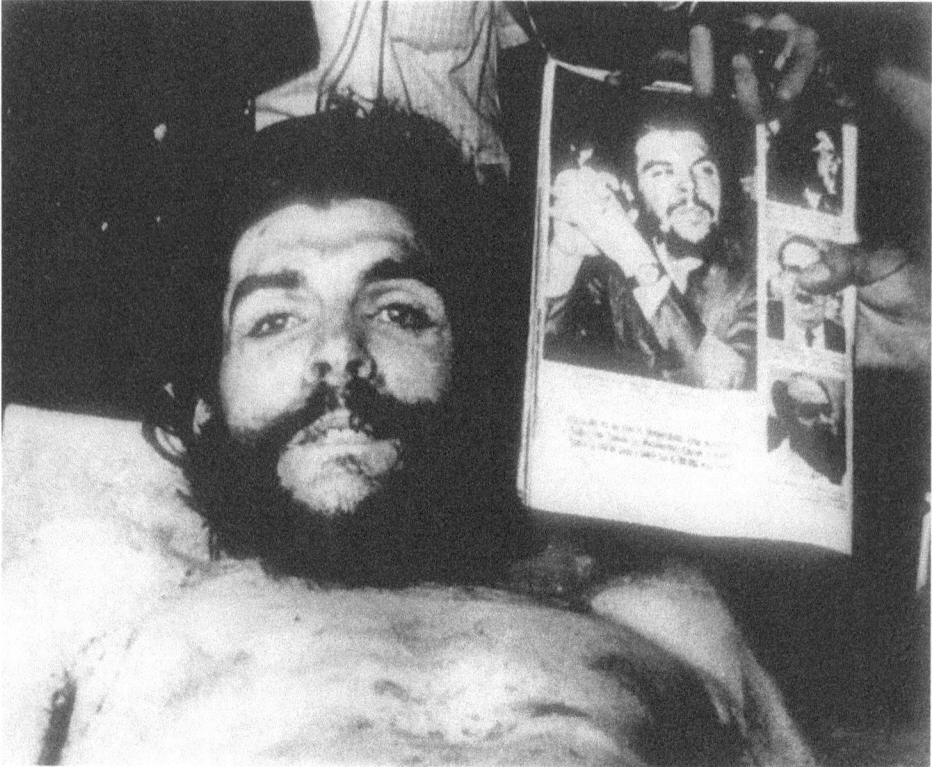

This famous Christ-like photo of Che Guevara in death, was first published in the United States on the cover of Ramparts magazine, creating sensation. Photographer unknown.

Alfredo Ovando Candia, head of the Bolivian armed forces, ordered the summary execution of the wounded Che Guevara, avoiding another trial such as that of the French revolutionary dilitante Regis Debray, which drew international attention. Photo courtesy of Freddy Alborta Trigo, La Paz photographer.

Antonio Arguedas, minister of state, who mailed Che Guevara's Bolivian diaries, which the military had tried to suppress to Cuba. Che Guevara and his little band had eluded some 5,000 Bolivian troops with U.S. advisors for a year. Antonio Arguedas, a civilian, took the rap to protect the prestige of the Bolivian military. Photo courtesy of Presencia.

President Juan Jose Torres, a populist, was one of the few Bolivian officers who courted labor, allowing all-labor Popular Assembly to meet for ten days. Before it could reconvene, however, Torres was overthrown with the most violence since the MNR revolt of 1952. He was later assassinated in exile in Argentina. Photo courtesy of Freddy Alborta Trigo.

Chapter Four

Argentina: Terror in the Global Village

The worst breakdown of law and violation of human rights in the hemisphere, initially almost unnoticed by the world press, occurred not in one of the "banana republics," in the popular view, but in one of the most highly sophisticated and well known countries of the region-Argentina-under military rule (1976–1983). The purge of political opponents, partly in reprisal for the urban guerrillas of preceding years, was called by the military itself the "dirty war," in which all means were justified—including kidnappings, detention in clandestine centers throughout the country, cut off from family or friends or legal counsel, tortured and killed. The number of victims, listed by the military as "disappeared," rose from 20,000 to 30,000 before the military were discredited by defeat in the Malvinas or Falkland Islands war in 1982, ending what can only be considered as political genocide or state terrorism.

The pitch of nationalist hysteria was voiced by General Iberico Saint-Jean who declared on May 26, 1977, one year after the military overthrew the incompetent Isabel Peron, "First we will kill all of the subversives; then we will kill their sympathizers; then . . . those who remain undecided, and finally we will kill the indifferent ones." This was a well planned and coldly executed effort to eradicate all opposition to the regime, Argentina's "ultimate solution" to perceived threats against the country's oligarchical social and economic structure.

How could this happen in a nation which had more libraries than any other Latin American country and had produced such great writers as Sarmiento and Jorge Luis Borges? (The latter, incidentally, like other citizens tired of the political turmoil, greeted the military officers of the 1976 coup as "gentlemen," but repelled by the outcome, admitted later that he had been "magnificently wrong.")

Meanwhile, the Argentine press, as the following selection indicates, simply looked the other way. Early on, foreign journalists heard rumors of detention centers but failed to follow up on the story. The Organization of American States sent an investigating commission and, although blocks and blocks of aggrieved Argentines lined up to testify, nothing came of it. It was the small group of mothers and other relatives of the disappeared who through their sheer persistence of silently walking in a circle on the esplanade in front of the Casa Rosada, the executive seat of government, every Thursday afternoon that finally caught the news media's attention. They became known as the Mothers of the Plaza de Mayo (the military called them the Mad Women of the Plaza de Mayo). They started in 1976 and are still marching today, until every human being is accounted for. I watched this demonstration of "people power," which caught the world's attention and admiration, one Thursday afternoon when I was in Buenos Aires in 1980 and was struck by the solemnity of the occasion. There was no chanting, no emotional outbursts as the Mothers simply walked silently around and around, some carrying photographs of their disappeared loved ones.

Thanks to the Mothers of the Plaza de Mayo, what was happening in Argentina finally goaded the foreign press to do its job and look into the matter. As criticism of the ruling military became more intense, they sought to divert public attention, first by hosting the World Cup soccer games, and then the ill-advised invasion of the Falkland Islands (see below) which was their undoing.

Like the Roman Catholic Church in the Spanish Civil War (1936 1939) which supported the fascist regime of Generalissimo Francisco Franco, the Argentine Church—with notable exceptions—came down on the side of the military. The amnesty granted to itself by the outgoing military was declared unconstitutional by the Argentine Supreme Court two years ago. This opened the way for prosecution of cases such as that of the three-judge tribunal which found the Rev. Christian von Wernich, tracked down in Chile by human rights activists, who had been police chaplain at one of the most notorious Argentine detention and torture centers, guilty of seven murders, 31 cases of torture and 42 kidnappings. He was sentenced to life imprisonment. The Navy Mechanics School was the largest clandestine torture center, where an estimated 4,500 prisoners were mistreated or murdered.

As the Argentine nation cleansed itself, various human rights groups sprang up to salvage what they could from this widespread tragedy. I remember most vividly what one of the directors of the Grandmothers of the Plaza de Mayo told me, "Young women apprehended by the police or military sometimes gave birth to their babies while in one of the detention centers. Their children frequently were given for 'adoption' to military families."

When I visited the offices of the Grandmothers of the Plaza de Mayo in 1983, I was overwhelmed by the walls covered with photographs of missing or unidentified children. The personnel there were working hard to identify these children and return them to their parents, assuming the latter were still alive. The personnel were using every scientific method possible, including DNA matching and medical records. It was almost a hopeless task, but those walls covered with pictures of children still haunt me.

Perhaps the most eloquent plea for sanity in Argentina came from the celebrated Peruvian novelist Mario Vargas Llosa, president of PEN, the world organization of writers, and perhaps best known in the United States for his novel, "Time of the Hero," who published an open letter to General Jorge Rafael Videla, who at that time headed the military regime in Argentina, on October 22, 1976, which protested in part:

> The list of actions taken against the basic principles of culture by the Argentine military covers a very wide spectrum: books seized from university and private libraries and then publicly burnt; the temporary or permanent closure of newspapers and journals and the establishment of a rigid censorship; the detention of writers and artists without specifying the charge and without bringing them before a judicial authority; harassment and closure of publishing houses; and the persecution of institutions dedicated to art and sociological research. Parallel with these official actions are those carried out by armed commandos in civilian dress, which your government up to now has neither prevented nor punished, and which have spread terror in many Argentine homes.

THE OTHER ARGENTINA

In some ways, Argentina has baffled North American observers ever since it was first settled in 1516 and, because of its remote location off the South Atlantic was the last of the three Spanish viceroyalties to be established (after Peru and Mexico City) before gaining independence in 1816. Baffling because its rich agricultural potential on the rolling Pampas, used mainly for grazing cattle and comprising most of the country, remains unused because of the internal feuding by the "beef barons" of the 19th century, who battled among themselves and also for supremacy over the port city of Buenos Aires, now three million strong in a country of 40 million people, producing political unrest that also stunted industrial development. (One is reminded of Bolivia with its untapped resources of the East, which has been described as "a beggar sitting on a throne of gold.")

As David Rock has pointed out in his history, *Argentina, 1516–1982*, in the first half of the 19th century, these rival *caudillos* (which he terms "provincial warlords") precipitated the "growth of segmentary, largely isolated local economies and a profusion of microstates." Thus, it was not until after 1850 that Argentina began to consolidate as a national state.

Still the old animosities between the plains and Buenos Aires continued, prompting James Scobie to title his history, *Argentina, A City and a Nation*. Yet Argentina had a homogeneous population after General Julio A. Roca waged a campaign of extermination against the remaining plains Indians (always sparse) in 1879, which boosted him into the presidency.

Also, there was a great influx of European immigrants—Italians and others—so that between 1871 and 1914 some 5.9 million immigrants flooded into Argentina, half of whom stayed, bringing with them ideas of socialism, anarchism, and syndicalism. Thus, in this regard, the culture of the Southern Cone—Argentina, Chile and Uruguay—is as much European as Latin American.

With the exception of Brazil, the economies of all the Latin American countries are centered in their capitals, all ringed with mushrooming shantytowns. According to the United Nations, one-third of the world's urban dwellers live in slums, burgeoning as the poor leave destitute rural areas seeking work in the cities. This number is expected to double by 2030, although it has begun to level off in Argentina. Put another way, Latin America was predominantly rural in 1950 but today is about 75 percent urban. The social effects of this migration have best been documented by Frantz Fanon in *The Wretched of the Earth* and in such revelations of the ravages of poverty as that of Carolina Maria Jesus, whose diary of life in a *favela* or shantytown in São Paulo, Brazil was published by an enterprising reporter in *O Cruzeiro*, Brazil's leading magazine, and eventually became a world classic as *Child of the Dark*.

Politically, much of the 20th century was dominated in Argentina by Juan Domingo Perón or his passionate followers, a populist and nationalistic movement as Perón and his first wife Evita tapped the power of the bereft, particularly the laborers who comprised the bulk of the *descamisados* (literally "shirtless ones"). Evita, the subject of a spectacular Broadway musical and film, was particularly adept at moving the multitudes before her death in 1952. General Perón himself, known abroad mainly for his running dispute with *La Prensa*, for many years the best known Latin American newspaper, ultimately confiscating it in 1951. In the Gainza Paz family for generations, it failed to see the reasons for the success of Juan and Eva Perón. The former went into eighteen years of exile after being overthrown in 1956, acquired two more wives and made "Isabel" (María Estela de Perón) his Vice-President when he returned to Argentina and was elected again before dying in 1974.

Peronism, although now split into three factions, is still vital enough to elect Cristina Fernández de Kirchener in 2007 as the second woman head of state in Latin America (after Michelle Bartelet of Chile). The former succeeded her incumbent husband, Nester Kirchener, who had pulled Argentina out of the financial collapse of 1991. But Cristina had been a senator from the provinces of Santa Cruz and Buenos Aires for ten years before her husband's rise to fame, so she could not be dismissed as riding on his coattails. Both came from the province of La Plata in Patagonia and were nicknamed by the Argentine people as "The Penguins."

Still the earlier and sordid past of the "dirty war" haunts Argentina. The country is trying to extradite María Estela de Perón from Spain, his Vice-President and third wife, overthrown by the military in 1976. She testified in exile in Spain that she had no connection with the notorious Triple-A (Argentine Anti-Communist Alliance), a paramilitary death squad dating from Perón's first period in office, and that she did not know what was being done in her name. But a judge in Mendoza, Argentina reminded her that she had been "the chief executive of the nation, and she signed decrees authorizing and used to abduct and later kill opponents to the Perón regime." (New York Times, January 13, 2007).

But it was not the breakdown of law or increasing international censure which finally did in the renegade Argentine military. It was their last desperate maneuver to divert attention from political problems at home by invading the Falkland Islands. General Leopoldo Galtieri launched the invasion on April 2, 1982. I do not presume to support or deny Argentina's claim to the islands, which had been a British Crown Colony since 1833, but they do lie only 300 miles off the Argentine coast in the South Atlantic, and are known in Argentina as the Malvinas, which is considerably closer to them than London. The islands were occupied by English and Scot sheep raisers, which prompted Prime Minister Margaret Thatcher, nicknamed the "Iron Lady" during the conflict, to dispatch 100 ships and 28,000 British troops to the area. The resulting two-month war, which cost the lives of 649 Argentine soldiers, 255 British troops, and three islanders. As John Smith, a Royal Navy sailor, later wrote in his account of the conflict, *74 Days*, "This was not a war waged at a distance. Sometimes there was fighting in your own garden."

Argentina and the United Kingdom resumed diplomatic relations in 1990, but the former has never relinquished its claim to the Malvinas. At the time of the fighting, Argentine citizens thought they were winning the war because of the misinformation fed them by a state-controlled press (only one Argentine journalist was allowed to go to the scene of the fighting). The rude shock of defeat hastened the end of the military regime, which was forced to call elections.

The islanders, who got full British citizenship out of the ordeal, did allow the establishment of a cemetery on a hillside overlooking Darwin for Argentine troops killed in battle. Many of the graves have inscriptions stating simply, "An Argentine soldier known only to God."

VEIL OF SILENCE: THE ARGENTINE PRESS AND THE DIRTY WAR, 1976–1983

Violence in Latin America seems endemic in the popular mind, but the stereotype became harsh reality in Argentina during the dirty war waged by the military regime against "subversives" between 1976 and 1983. This resulted in the most severe onslaught against the press by any government in hemispheric history, with 84 journalists among the 8,960 persons originally documented as killed or missing in 1983 after the military left power (CONADEP, 1984: 372–374).

The true dimensions of this miniature holocaust, however, may never be known, Emilio F. Mignone, president of the Center for Legal and Social Studies in Buenos Aires, the most reliable source for human rights statistics in Argentina, believes that the number of the disappeared will reach 20,000 when all of the evidence is sifted and those in remote corners of the country—hitherto afraid to speak out—come forward (interview, July 25, 1990). When Adolfo Francisco Scilingo, a former lieutenant commander in the Argentine navy, admitted in 1995 that 1,500 to 2,000 live and drugged bodies of victims had been jettisoned into the Atlantic from planes, the *Los Angeles Times* (March 13, 1995) and other newspapers revived earlier speculation that the final toll would go as high as 30,000 persons.

"One [victim] is too many," says Catarina Guagnini, of the Argentine human rights group Families of the Disappeared and Detained for Political Reasons, formed in 1976. She lost a daughter and two sons—one a correspondent for *El País*, the distinguished Spanish newspaper (interview, July 5, 1990). Young men and women like her children were abducted from their homes or workplaces or on the streets, and most were never seen again. In the face of seemingly indifferent or uninformed public opinion, they were held incommunicado in clandestine detention centers, charged with nothing, tortured, and killed. Their bodies were buried in mass graves in obscure cemeteries, dumped in the ocean from navy planes, or thrown onto the streets—supposedly as victims of "shootouts" between the police and urban guerrilla groups.

The victims of this military terror included lawyers who defended political prisoners and psychiatrists who treated those who had been tortured. Mainly they were students, labor organizers, members of human rights groups, and other community activists. Actors, singers, painters, and others in the arts and education whose voices of conscience deplored Argentina's unjust social structure also were targeted. As Clara de Israel, who directs a neighborhood center named for her disappeared lawyer daughter, Teresa Israel, puts it, "The best of a whole generation was exterminated" (interview, July 16, 1990).

During this well-organized and disciplined political purge, the Argentine press was, at first glance, strangely silent. With two notable exceptions, the English-language *Buenos Aires Herald*, not deemed a threat because of its small circulation and foreign language, and *La Opinión* of Jacobo Timerman until his arrest in 1977, the print and electronic media simply did not report what was going on. A veil of silence dropped over the mainstream Argentine press in a country once known for its sharp newspaper criticism of authoritarian governments. Why this more recent know-nothing attitude on the part of the press?

Was it fear of those military figures who seized control of the Argentine government in 1976? Some 400 journalists, along with many of their fellow citizens—those who could afford it—fled the country. Others, such as Francisco Eduardo Marín of *La Nación*, were dismissed from newspaper staffs because of their political views. Was it simply indifference on the part of both the press and public, a matter of conveniently looking the other way? Communications scholars have long debated whether the media are influential in shaping society—for better or worse—or simply reflect the values of that society. When a BBC correspondent asked the news editor of *La Nación* why his publication had nothing to say about the disappearances, he replied, "Our readers are not interested" (*Index on Censorship*, March 1980, 46). Or was this silence out-and-out complicity between the military and the established Argentine press? Although fear and indifference were undoubtedly part of the equation, most of the Argentine press remained silent out of sheer self-interest. They were shielding their own social and economic flanks, whether protecting government advertising revenues or simply not wishing to disturb the social structure of which they were a part. Few in Argentina at the time could claim to be unaware that something was happening, given the magnitude of these events. As Juan E. Méndez of the Americas Watch Committee notes, the Argentine military conducted the dirty war on a scale "that finds no precedent in Argentine history and with a ferocity comparable to any of the tragedies experienced by human kind subsequent to World War II." And George A. López, an expert on state terrorism, adds, "The systematic disappearance of large numbers of presumed adversaries (and often their relatives, who asked authorities about the whereabouts of their kin) by the Argentine military rulers of 1976–1981 constitutes an occurrence unprecedented in the Americas."

Publicly, the military only admitted shortly before leaving office in 1983 that 2,050 "terrorists" had been killed by government forces in 742 armed confrontations between 1973 and 1979. The final statement by the military—until 1995—also claimed that "the strictest secrecy had to be imposed upon the information covering military actions." Privately, however, the military seemed to encourage rumors to implant terror, intimidation, and obedience to the regime. As a naval officer told Jacobo Timerman, the military was looking for a "final solution" so "there'll be fear for several generations." The military, he said, would eliminate not only those guilty of violence but "their relatives too—they must be eradicated—and also those who remembered their names."

Perhaps the most balanced view of the dirty war, however, when the facts began to emerge, came from Ernesto Sábato, the well-known Argentine public figure selected by President Raúl Alfonsín in 1983 to head the Comisión Nacional sobre la Desaparición de Personas (National Commission on the Disappearance of Persons—CONADEP): "In the years that preceded the coup d'etat of 1976 [in which the military overthrew Isabel Perón], there were acts of terrorism which no civilized community could justify. Citing these deeds, the military dictatorship unleashed a terrorism infinitely worse because the army, a gigantic power with the total impunity allowed under an absolute state, started an infernal witch-hunt in which not only the terrorists but also thousands and thousands of innocent persons paid with their lives."

PERÓN AND THE PRESS

Since no national press system exists in a historical or social vacuum, it is necessary to examine briefly the roots of the society that countenanced the dirty war and the print and electronic news media that did not object. The Argentine sociologist Gino Germani has identified as the two most important forces in the 20th-century history of his country the growing industrial bourgeoisie after 1930 and the concomitantly rising urban proletariat. Both wrested political power from the colonial and 19th-century oligarchy of *estancieros* (large landowners). One of these "beef barons," José Clemente Paz, founded *La Prensa*, destined to be Argentina's best-known newspaper, in dominant Buenos Aires in 1869. Established to referee in gentlemanly fashion the intramural elite political contests of its time, *La Prensa* was not sympathetic to social changes.

Nevertheless, with its emphasis also on foreign news, *La Prensa* was an advance over earlier Argentine newspapers, which had been filled mainly with polemics and philosophical discussions. Ezequiel Paz, son of the founder, regarded the newspaper as a chronicle, emphasizing news rather than views. But it still remained implicitly political with elite agendas, on the model of U.S. newspapers, rather than the explicitly political orientation of much of the European press and some Buenos Aires newspapers. Actually, in contrast to most of Latin America, Argentina had wide freedom of the press after the Supreme Court decision of 1866 prohibited the federal government from enacting laws limiting that freedom. This decision was not reversed until 1932.

By then, other forces were penetrating Argentine society, notably intervention by the military, always regarded as the "tutelary" institution in Latin America. The French scholar Alain Rouquié has amply demonstrated the development of a "military subsystem" in Argentina that allied itself with the urban middle class after the initial failure of Peronism (1946–1955). This alliance ensured the military's own prerogatives and fought off attempts at radical social change by Peronists or others. Rouquié sees the political instability and fragmentation of Argentina since 1930 as a "crisis of participation" by those excluded from real political power.

Partly as a backlash to dissident underground newspapers of the entire range of the political spectrum, mainstream Argentine publishers cast their lot with the military, viewed as preservers of law and order. In their view, what other choice did they have? Since the benchmark of 1930, when the tentative reforms of Hipólito Irigoyen triggered a military coup, Argentina has been wracked by five other successful military interventions. In fact, when the elected civilian President Raúl Alfonsín was inaugurated on December 10, 1983, after the dirty war, Argentina had experienced only 13 years of civilian rule in the preceding 50 years.

The established Argentine press, especially *La Prensa* and *La Nación* (founded by Bartolomé Mitre in 1870), feared the new group of military officers that came to power in 1943. Colonel Juan Domingo Perón, elected president in 1946, based his power on the laboring masses of Argentina's *descamisados* (shirtless ones) and recognized the importance of the press for marshaling them in his *justicialista* revolution. Perón's running battle with *La Prensa*, culminating in that newspaper's expropriation in 1951,is well known. Less well known was the Peronist Congress's closure of some 70 provincial newspapers and Eva Perón's purchase of three Buenos Aires papers, including *Democracia*, which became the government's spokesman. The expropriated *La Prensa* later served that function until Perón's ouster in 1955, when it was returned to the Paz family.

The threat of heavy-handed governmental interference with the press of this period caused the news media to be more cautious. Even before the return to power by Perón in 1973 after 18 years in exile, tighter press restrictions were evident. A decree of February 1970, for instance, made the Ministry of Government responsible for "orientation and control" of all radio and television stations in Argentina, which were also obliged to preserve "the national style of life" in all broadcasts.

In his second term in office, which ended with his death in 1974, Perón tried to make Argentina a hermetically sealed society, cushioning the shock waves of foreign news and opinion. A decree of August 1973 prohibited international news agencies from distributing news about Argentina produced elsewhere. The wire services UPI and AP were banned altogether in 1974, and, according to Franklin Rawson Paz, director of *La Nación* (interview, July 4, 1983), Perón closed two newspapers—*Noticias* and *El Mundo*.

Yet the return of Perón with his vice president and third wife, María Estela Martínez (Isabel), to the Argentine political arena sparked a flurry of publications. Every group aspired to have its say, from mimeographed newsletters to glossy magazines. Within a population of 25 million in 1973 there were 117 morning dailies, 54 evening newspapers, and 500 magazines. Authorities warned the established press to ignore or minimize terrorist activities, whether by the Peronist Montoneros or the Marxist-Leninist Ejército Revolucionario del Pueblo (People's Revolutionary Army—ERP). The press of the left—whether the ERP's *El Combatiente* or the more widely circulated Montoneros' daily *Noticias* (150,000) or weekly *El Descamisado* (100,000)—was so vigorous that it brought down official retaliation. In September 1974 a new antisubversion law provided up to five years in prison for any journalist disseminating information "altering or eliminating institutional order."

One by one the opposition newspapers were closed during the administration of Isabel Perón (1974–1976), perhaps an object lesson for the mainstream press, which said nothing about the closures. In fact, they were forbidden even to mention the proscribed Montoneros or ERP by name. The veil of silence had begun to descend.

THE CASE OF TIMERMAN

When the Argentine military overthrew the figurehead government of Isabel Perón on March 21, 1976, the way was opened for full-scale repression. The first prominent figure to feel the officers' wrath was Jacobo Timerman, publisher and editor of *La Opinión*, a liberal newspaper that had raised its voice against the increasing military terror. Timerman was no newcomer to

Argentine journalism. He had founded the reviews *Primera Plana* in 1962 and *Confirmado* in 1965 and the morning daily *La Opinión* itself in 1971. On March 24, 1977, *La Opinión* published a supplement entitled "The Silence of the Politicians," attacking them for their complacency in the face of the increasing violation of human rights by the ruling military. When Timerman was arrested on April 14, 1977, the military claimed that his main partner at *La Opinión*, David Graiver—who had died a year earlier in a plane crash—had laundered US $17 million of Montoneros ransom money through the family bank. The implication planted by the military was that *La Opinión* had actually been founded with Montoneros money. The publisher himself never addressed this charge in his *Prisoner Without a Name, Cell Without a Number*, but he testified when finally brought before a military court that the media scandal against the Graiver family "could have concealed a maneuver to buy their holdings at a low price."

Although anti-Semitism, always latent in Argentine life, undoubtedly played a part in the persecution of Timerman, the only Jewish editor in Buenos Aires, the main reason was his opposition to the dirty war. As Colonel Ramón Juan Alberto Camps, chief of police of Buenos Aires province, later tried and convicted of atrocities, declared in 1982, "If anyone had to be pointed out as one of those principally responsible for the cultural subversion which armed the consciences of the guerrillas, that would be Jacobo Timerman." Camps added, in defending the military's actions, "From its beginning *La Opinión* was converted into an enterprise of cultural dissolution [which was] the most powerful that marxism counted upon in our country."

One index of the close ties between the oligarchical press and the ruling military was that Máximo Gainza, fourth-generation publisher of *La Prensa*, collaborated with Colonel Camps in writing the book *Caso Timerman: Punto final (The Timerman Case: Full Stop)* in 1982.

They concluded, "In respect [to military excesses], we should remember that it is lawful in wartime to do whatever is necessary for the defense of the endangered public welfare." For Timerman, this meant being confined incommunicado in a tiny cell in one of the clandestine detention centers, charged with nothing and repeatedly tortured. He was held for more than 40 months, partly under house arrest, before finally being cleared by a military court and ordered released by the Supreme Court. He was freed only after enormous international pressure—which probably saved his life—including that by Secretary of State Cyrus Vance of the Jimmy Carter administration. Timerman was stripped of his Argentine citizenship and property without compensation and went into exile in Israel. Although he did not revive *La Opinión* when he returned to Argentina in 1983, he became editor-in-chief of the Buenos Aires daily *La Razón*.

MAINSTREAM SILENCE

The *Buenos Aires Herald* was the only other Argentine newspaper to speak out against the dirty war consistently as it unfolded. It had a small circulation—only 16,000 in 1983—and reached only an English-reading public. *La Prensa* did publish 2,500 names of the disappeared in an advertisement in June 1978 and again a pamphlet of 5,600 names in 1980, when the peak years of the terror from 1976 to 1979 had passed. But few Argentine newspapers reported the disappearances or analyzed what lay behind them. As the Argentine journalist Eduardo Crawley has noted, "The rest of the press [other than *La Opinión* and the *Herald*] remained completely silent, as did the politicians, and the great mass of the population preferred not to know." Andrew Graham-Yooll, a writer for the *Buenos Aires Herald* who went into exile in 1976, adds that investigative journalism was out of the question, because such a fragile balance between the military regime and the national papers or large provincial dailies permitted no delving into any issue.

Was it complicity between the large newspapers and the military that invoked this silence? Rodolfo Audi, head of the 18,000-member Argentine Federation of Press Workers calls it collaboration to preserve the status quo. The government repression during the dirty war, Audi believes, "was to eliminate the entire field of independent communication. The established newspapers became accomplices in the process" (interview, July 10, 1990). Jorge Lanata, director of *Página/12*, the leading interpretive newspaper of Buenos Aires, agrees with this assessment, adding that the major newspapers were literally partners of the government at that time. Because Perón had once cut off the supply of paper or limited the size of editions to manipulate the press, *Clarín*, *La Nación*, and *La Prensa* had joined with the government to form Papel Prensa, which regulated the flow of that vital paper for all publications (Jorge Lanata, letter to Committee to Protect Journalists, September 8, 1993). Thus, the three major papers of Argentina had a direct interest in the survival of the military regime. Moreover, since the regime still owned about 40 percent of industry before privitization began, government advertising was not to be offended. For publishing its pamphlet of the names of 5,600 disappeared in 1980, *La Prensa* suffered an advertising boycott by the military authorities in 1980–1981, according to Máximo Gainza, the last of the Paz-Gainza family to direct the newspaper before it was sold after 1990 (interview, July 12, 1990).

Other responsible observers saw links between the Argentine government and the Argentine press culminating in the see-no-evil attitude that made the dirty war possible if not inevitable. Early in the tragedy, the Argentine Commission on Human Rights in 1977 characterized *La Prensa* as "spokesman of the

Argentine oligarchy and of the principal transnational enterprises." Although the newspaper did speak out against the wave of anti-Semitism unleashed by the unstable political situation, it was also described by the commission as "one of the most decided defenders [of the military]." The commission also condemned "the marked official tendency of the great newspapers," magazines, and radio and television, the latter two media having been nationalized in 1974 (Comisión Argentina por los Derechos Humanos, 1977: 121, 117).

JOURNALISM UNDER SIEGE

Concretely, how did the military control and manipulate the Argentine press after gaining power in 1976? First of all, the military press director issued notices, with no letter or authorizing signature, to all news editors, disguising the fact that it was a notification of official censorship. It stated: "As of today [April 22, 1976], it is forbidden to inform, comment or make reference to the death of subversive elements and/or the armed and security forces in these incidents, unless they are reported by a responsible official source" (quoted in Graham-Yooll, 1981: 93). This warning also proscribed news about missing persons and victims of kidnappings. The *Buenos Aires Herald* printed this notice on its front page in protest, but only one other newspaper mentioned it. *Clarín*, indeed, ran a full-page story asserting that there were no restrictions on the press in Argentina. The purpose of this anonymous notice, of course, was to induce self-censorship. Can one blame the journalists who proceeded cautiously? As Graham-Yooll, who has shared the painful experience of his Argentine exile with us, described the situation in May 1976, "The immorality of self-censorship became less reprehensible with the growing number of journalists killed" (1981: 93).

The mainstream press itself condoned the military repression. *Clarín*, for instance (October 23, 1982), censured the "means of social communication . . . [which print] disruptive preachments, pernicious and destabilizing, that aid the reactivation of subversive ideologies." Other major newspapers, directed to the middle and upper classes, also defended the economic interests of those groups, according to Lauro Fernán Laiño, editorial director of *La Razón* (interview, July 7, 1990).

Connivance with the military also occurred at a more personal level, as officials of the regime paid bribes or *chivos* (literally, goats) to individual journalists to get something into the media or to keep it out. An accepted custom in many parts of Latin America, this was another means of control wielded by the military over the press. For instance, Miguel Angel López Ormeño, news director of a small radio station in Buenos Aires, augmented his meager US $400 monthly salary with US $150–200 in *chivos* (interview, July 10, 1990).

Nevertheless, it was the major voices of the Argentine press that tended to be sycophants of whoever was in power. Robert Cox, former editor of the *Buenos Aires Herald*, whose own reporting of the disappearances won him the María Moors Cabot prize, awarded annually by Columbia University for courage in inter-American journalism, noted that *Gente*, for example, the most widely circulated newspaper in Argentina, essentially fawns upon whatever faction is in power. During the Isabel Perón government, *Gente* published stories and pictures designed to please officialdom, but when the military usurped that constitutional government the newsmagazine displayed marked enthusiasm for the military. Cox concluded, "To a greater or lesser degree, depending upon economic interests and political loyalties, the entire Argentine press does the same."

Moreover, the Argentine press reacted with delay—if it reacted at all—to the dirty-war story. As Cox also points out, "For some years now, reality in Argentina has been possible only after the event . . . Public indignation, therefore, is always being whipped into a frenzy long after the die has been cast. The media's coverage of [state] terrorism followed this pattern." Ritualistic violence was not for public view until it was safely in the past.

At the same time, newspaper offices in much of Latin America are clearinghouses for human problems, and it was natural for family members of the disappeared to turn to the press for help in locating them—and not by paid advertisements. These free notices seeking information were published only in the *Buenos Aires Herald* and, before its confiscation, *La Opinión*. Ronald Hansen, then managing editor of the *Herald*, said that the established press shunted such solicitants to the never-ending labyrinth of government offices (interview, July 8, 1983). Robert Cox, editor of the *Herald*, personally tried to trace as many of these cases as possible before death threats ultimately forced him and his family to leave Argentina.

Another pernicious effect of the silence of the mainstream press was that seven years slipped by with no adequate chronicle of Argentine history. Divorced from reality, whether by choice or ineptness, the press buried its head in the sand, hoping the unpleasantness would go away. Resurrecting the facts after 1983 has proved as difficult as identifying the bones. As Graham Yooll comments, "With the end of dictatorship, [Argentina] is trying to reconstruct a history of which it has kept no records."

MEDIA BREAKTHROUGH

By default, it was the international media that first brought world attention to the plight of the disappeared, and it was a "media event" of the highest order that did so. In April 1977, shortly after the arrest of Timerman and the confiscation of *La Opinión*, a group of mothers and other relatives of the victims of the dirty war began marching for an hour every Thursday afternoon in front of the Casa Rosada, the government executive offices. They demanded to know the whereabouts of their loved ones. Their remarkable persistence also caused them to march against the pardons of convicted officers after 1983 and in protest of the fact that others were never brought to trial. They are still demonstrating to this day for those unaccounted for. Known as the Mothers of the Plaza de Mayo, they were derisively called "the Mad Women of the Plaza de Mayo" by officials at the time. One of the Mothers claimed in 1990 that 90 percent of the judges who sat during the military period continued in their posts (Juana Meller de Pargament, interview, July 18, 1990).

There are no secrets in the global village. Because of the publicity generated by the Mothers of the Plaza de Mayo, a decisive breakthrough came in 1978, when the Organization of American States sent its Commission on Human Rights to Argentina for a three-week investigation at the request of the Argentine government. More than 2,000 persons waited to testify in a line stretching five blocks from the building where the hearings were being held. Still, the Argentine press did not give wide currency to these proceedings and would not cover the story until state terrorism was in sharp decline after 1980.

As Argentina reaped an increasingly bad international press, regime officials sought to divert attention from domestic matters by hosting the World Soccer Championship games in 1978 and later occupying the Malvinas/ Falklands in 1982. An Argentine observer called these "the two most detestable mass manipulations of the regime" to divert attention from a shattered economy and the rising storm over human rights abuses.

Government by public relations was nothing new in Latin America, and the press generally did not see through it. The regime of Fulgencio Batista in Cuba (1934–1959) hired Edmund Chester, a former CBS executive, to prop up its sagging image, and René Barrientos in Bolivia (1964–1969) allegedly paid US $280,000 in 1965—more than the entire budget for the Ministry of Mines and Petroleum—to the U.S. public relations firm of Hamilton Wright Organization to burnish his military image.

An Argentine researcher has found that the military regime there counted on the resources of five national public relations or advertising agencies after the Department of Psychological Action (Propaganda) was created under the Secretariat of Public Information. Two of these firms were associated with U.S. agencies—Ogilvi and Mather, and Grey Advertising Inc. Young and Rubicam also operated independently in Argentina. Between 1975 and 1976, money spent for publicity increased 60.2 percent, and in 1979 alone US $1,060 million were spent on national advertising and public relations (although it is not clear how much of this went to promote national industry and how much for political purposes).

Taking a cue from public relations advisers, General Albano Harguinde-guy, minister of government, held a series of "dialogues" with the Argentine press that extended more than four months in 1980. Partly as a result of these exchanges, the military announced in May 1981 that, as a move toward decentralization, each government office would deal directly with the press (*Convicción*, May 20, 1981). Some took a jaundiced view of such proceedings, however. When the minister of government called 18 women journalists to his office for a conference, one of them, Monica d'Anvers, said, "I think that in Argentina we are not speaking the truth because we are afraid, because we shut things up" (*Clarín*, July 13, 1980).

It was defeat at the hands of Britain in the South Atlantic, however, that finally forced the military to step down. With strict censorship imposed during the war, most Argentines believed that they were actually winning the Malvinas conflict. The people learned only what the government wanted them to know through the four nationalized television channels and 90 radio stations. Once again, the regime sought to manipulate the press totally. Only one Argentine journalist, Nicolás Kazantzew of Channel 7, was allowed to go to the scene of the fighting. As Juan Carlos Romero, subdirector of Salta's *El Tribuno*, noted, when their fighting men began coming home as released prisoners of war, Argentines were astonished and embittered (interview, July 6, 1983).

After being discredited in the Malvinas defeat, the military called for elections on October 30, 1983, the first in ten years, but before turning control over to civilians it sought to cover its tracks. At first, in 1979 the military decreed that no one had disappeared—there were simply "unregistered deaths." This law allowed a judge to declare someone "presumably dead" after an absence of three months rather than the three years prescribed in the civil code, allowing the government to close the books on the disappearances more quickly.

The cover-up gained momentum when General Roberto Eduardo Viola declared in May 1979 that those who had disappeared were "absent forever." Again, Viola told the armed forces in May 1980 that they had nothing to fear. "The tribunals of Nuremberg were only for the conquered," he said. "One does not ask for an accounting from a victorious army." On August 12, 1980, some 175 Argentines from all walks of life signed a newspaper advertisement condemning the violation of human rights in Argentina. But in April 1983 the outgoing military decreed that all measures used during the campaign against "subversion" were "acts of service" carried out in the line of duty. A self-proclaimed amnesty in September 1983 sought to prohibit prosecution of any military person for acts committed during the reign of terror.

TRIALS AND PARDONS

In the face of mounting international condemnation of Argentina, President Raúl Alfonsín, installed in office in December 1983, immediately submitted proposals to raise the sentence for torture to life imprisonment, put military courts under civilian rule, and repeal the amnesty the military had granted itself in September (*New York Times*, December 17, 1983). Even more significant, on December 15, 1983, Alfonsín established the National Commission on the Disappearance of Persons (CONADEP), headed by the respected statesman Ernesto Sábato, to investigate the matter. Given eight months to complete its work, CONADEP's 50,000-page report urged the prosecution of 1,351 military men and police who had conducted their illegal activities in 365 clandestine detention centers.

Meanwhile, the Argentine press had clambered aboard the new bandwagon of uncovering atrocities and reporting the subsequent trials. It seems reasonable to assert that most Argentines were surprised only by the scope of the CONADEP findings and later trials. As CONADEP reported, "The whole country knew that detentions were being carried out, but it was prohibited to know how many there were, who they were, and where they were taken" (CONADEP, 1984: 368). Rumor is always more damaging than fact, but it had been to the advantage of Argentina's military rulers to let rumors proliferate to implant terror in the general populace.

With worldwide attention riveted on Argentina, some 700 journalists descended on Buenos Aires to cover the trials. The Mothers of the Plaza de Mayo declared, "We Mothers . . . [have] suffered in our own flesh the vileness of that despicable press that today pretends to be democratic but only wants to make business with our pain and with the horror of the tragedy of the 'disappeared'."

The trials began on April 22, 1985, and lasted 78 days. The nine junta members during the early military regimes were not charged with "genocide" or "crimes against humanity" but with 711 specific violations of Argentine law. Five of the nine—including former military presidents Jorge Rafael Videla and Roberto Eduardo Viola—were found guilty, with sentences ranging from life imprisonment to four and a half years in prison. In a separate trial, Ramón J. Camps was sentenced to 25 years in prison for human rights abuses.

These successful prosecutions caused other trials to proliferate, to the great distress of the Argentine military, sparking three abortive uprisings against the civilian administration of Raúl Alfonsín. Under this pressure, he began accommodating the military with the Ley de Punto Final (Full

Stop Law) of December 1986. Under its terms, there were to be no new prosecutions after 60 days. The government expected no more than 30 or 40 new cases to be brought during this grace period, but actually there were more than 400. Secondly, the government of Alfonsín approved the Ley de Obediencia Debida (Due Obedience Law) of June 1987, which exempted from prosecution for violation of human rights all lower-ranking officers and others following orders.

Because of the catastrophic slide of the Argentine economy, Alfonsín stepped down five months before the expiration of his term. He was followed by Carlos Saúl Menem, a Peronist elected in 1989 and reelected in 1995. Intermittently imprisoned by the military himself, Menem issued his first pardon on October 6, 1989, for all those "in process"—awaiting trial or being tried. And on December 29, 1990, he wiped the slate clean by pardoning all those in prison, more than 200 military men and 60 alleged guerrillas who had never been brought to trial (*New York Times*, October 11 and 12, 1989).

Human rights groups in Argentina were outraged, and an independent poll revealed that 63 percent of the Argentine public opposed these pardons. Carlos Zamorano of the Argentine League for the Rights of Man, for example, called the pardons "a grave injustice to the judicial power" (interview, July 20, 1990), and Alfredo Pedro Bravo of the Permanent Assembly for Human Rights denounced the final pardons as "a barbarity" (interview, July 12, 1990). Enrique Pochat of the Ecumenical Movement for Human Rights, an alliance of Catholic and Protestant churches formed in 1976 to meet the social needs of families of the disappeared, said that two goals were driving these human rights groups: the quest for truth and reconstructing history—the deep-seated need to find out what had happened to every one of the disappeared—and justice, not vengeance. "The Argentine people suffered the law of the jungle," he maintains. "We cannot walk away from that" (interview, July 23, 1990).

The pardons brought back the foreign journalists, prompting Catarina Guagnini to declare, "Now there are heaps of journalists here. Where were you when we needed you?" (interview, July 5, 1990). The difficulty with crisis reporting—whether of the dirty war itself or of the ensuing trials and pardons—is that attention is focused on something only when it surfaces, and in this case the deep undercurrents of Argentine life remained hidden from public scrutiny. As for the Argentine press itself, it should come as no surprise that not one of the leaders of these eight human rights groups interviewed in Buenos Aires in 1990 looked to the Argentine press for help. On the contrary, they charged that the country's press had merely seized upon the trials and pardons for sensational exploitation.

CONCLUSIONS

The dirty war in Argentina was not, as some have indicated, a hysterical response by the military or ideological intoxication. It was a coldly calculated policy to obliterate those active in seeking a better life for all Argentines. As General Jorge Rafael Videla declared in 1975, "As many people will die in Argentina as necessary to restore order." The simplistic military mind, which sees force as the ultimate solution to all problems, had its roots deep in the Perón era, when the Argentine press experienced governmental force and manipulation. As Secretary of State Dean Acheson once phrased it, "Perón was a fascist and a dictator detested by all good men—except Argentines." He took on an oligarchical press and rode roughshod over newspapers from *La Prensa* on down, establishing a subservient role for the press from which it has never recovered. The circulation of *La Prensa*, which largely ignored social problems, fell from 400,000 when it was expropriated in 1951 to 80,000 in 1983 (Gainza interview, July 12, 1983).

The silence of the mainstream Argentine press during the dirty war itself raises some disturbing questions for which there are no easy answers, but the links of the Argentine press with the military authorities may shed some light on the problem. First, how could a nation as cultured as Argentina, which has produced world-renowned writers and humanitarians, fall into the trap of the dirty war, countenancing torture, murder, and other widespread abuses in the name of a higher good? The public seemed not to want to know what was happening, and in this regard it was as culpable as the press itself. In view of this indifference, little by little the failure of the Argentine press to unmask these crimes metamorphosed from complacency into complicity.

And those journalists who would not go along were targeted. As the report of CONADEP pointed out: "It was not by coincidence or error that the number of victims is so high [in the press] in relation to [other] professionals. By attacking the vast field of culture, always viewed with jealousy by dictatorships, it is evident that [the military] aimed to silence a social group of great importance in order to pull up by the roots any public questioning" (CONADEP, 1984: 367). Although on a smaller scale, this amounted to the "political and economic cleansing of the press" that Oron J. Hale has traced in the Third Reich. He also noted that Hitler himself singled out for destruction what he called "overeducated intellectuals."

As in Germany, the breakdown of communications in Argentina led to a breakdown in society itself. While the Latin American press in general has not realized its potential adversarial role toward government, this was not entirely true in Argentina, where a significant portion of the press had opposed Perón. The military in 1976 inherited a press to be reckoned with, which is why it co-opted the major newspapers and radio and television stations, stressing their common ideological grounds. Dissident journalists were purged by the news media themselves, and self-censorship imposed by very real threats kept others in line. The mechanism for accomplishing all this was quite simple—exaggerating the threat of the "terrorists" so that people would accept harsh military measures to combat them.

How real was the guerrilla threat to Argentine society? The Center for Legal and Social Studies maintains that at their peak the insurgent forces did not number more than 2,000, of whom only 20 percent were armed. Facing them were armed forces and police of 200,000 effectives backed up by one of the most sophisticated military machines in Latin America. Others also believed that the guerrilla threat was a straw man used to eliminate peaceful reformers. Carlos Zamorano of the Argentine League for the Rights of Man states flatly, "War against the guerrillas was a lie. Terror wasn't necessary. The military themselves did not believe in any threat" (interview, July 20, 1990). Walter Little of the University of Liverpool has described the strategy of the Montoneros and the ERP as follows: "On the whole it has been instrumental, selective violence and has not been terrorist in the proper meaning of the term. Terrorism by the left consists of attacks upon civilian innocents, not so much with the object of demonstrating to the regime that their will to resist is undiminished, but rather to demonstrate to the citizenry that the regime is not capable of protecting their lives or property" (quoted in Graham-Yooll, 1984: 10). Thus, after the "terrorists" were annihilated, the military turned to the social groups believed to sympathize with them—journalists, unionists, students, creative artists, and community activists—because they would provide the peripheral support for future attempts to change Argentina's lopsided social structure.

One may ask why the clash between the Argentine military and those who disappeared was so severe in relation to other Latin American confrontations. Right-wing death squads wreaked havoc in Guatemala and El Salvador, and many died by the Shining Path in Peru. But the answer is the overwhelmingly higher technology at the command of those who made up the military subsystem in Argentine society. The country was divided into military zones, and the slaughter was thoroughly systematized.

Nevertheless, the military in Argentina needed the cooperation of key sectors of society—including journalism and the church—to carry out its social-economic "purification." Many of the officers were sons of the elite who saw their status threatened. And the military was exceedingly thin-skinned about its class status. One issue of the magazine *La Semana* was confiscated, for example, because it published a cover photograph of a woman TV personality wearing an officer's cap (Guarescha interview, July 13, 1983).

Finally, there were the economic interests of the press itself. Publishing newspapers is big business. Some do it for political power, but most entrepreneurs go into it to make money, and they do not want to see their multimillion-dollar investments threatened by societal change or have government-sponsored advertising withdrawn.

The audience of any mass communications system must also be taken into account. Those who read, listen, or watch—or decline to do so—determine in part what is presented to them. The Argentine press during the dirty war was so effective in a massive cover-up that it took 13 years for any commanding officer to admit—even after the trials and pardons—that abduction, torture, and murder had indeed been carried out on a wide scale. It was not until 1995 that General Martín Balza, chief of staff, admitted in a television interview that the army had "employed illegitimate methods, including the suppression of life, to obtain information" (*New York Times*, April 26, 1995).

But what actually caused the dirty war itself is open to question. There was a confluence of currents of thought and action at a deadly time. On the one hand was the Argentine military's desire for revenge against those who had dared challenge its authority in the 1960s and early 1970s. On the other hand, as in much of Latin America, the Argentine military regarded itself as the tutelary institution or custodian of the national destiny. In the mid-1960s the concept became prevalent among the Argentine military that national security was inextricably coupled with economic development, as formulated in the National Security Doctrine. Thus, the role of the military became tied to the regime's preservation against "internal enemies" no matter what the cost.

General Balza's statement reopened old wounds and caused the human rights organizations to press harder for a full accounting—and no pardons. As Hebe de Bonafini, current head of the Mothers of the Plaza de Mayo, declared, "Pardon is divine for those who still believe in God, but we don't pardon" (*New York Times*, March 25, 1995).

In the last analysis, how can the historian quantify silence? How does one measure words unspoken? Robert Cox has titled his personal observations of the tragedy of the Argentine press and the country as a whole during the dirty war with the philosophical concept of *The Sound of One Hand Clapping* (1980). Despite the perseverance of a few courageous voices, Argentina is still waiting for the other hand to clap.

(Jerry W. Knudson, "Veil of Silence, The Argentine Press and the 'Dirty War.'" Reprinted by permission of *Latin American Perspectives*, 24:6 (November 1997), 93–112.)

Chapter Five

Chile: The Nation that Survived

When Michelle Bachelet was inaugurated the first woman President of Chile on March 11, 2006, she seemed to some an anomaly in many ways. An agnostic in a country where the Catholic Church has been powerful enough to block the legalization of divorce until two years ago, Bachelet was also a pediatrician and former Minister of Health, the divorced mother of three children (the last one "natural," in Latin American terminology, not "illegitimate").

Most astonishingly, although she had only five years of political experience, these included two years as Minister of Defense, commanding that bastion of masculinity, the Chilean armed forces. She sought the position in an attempt to bring about a reconciliation between the Chilean people and the military. The wounds were still deep after the abuses by the armed forces under the dictatorship of General Augusto Pinochet (1973–1990), who died in 2007 while under house arrest, too ill to stand trial for charges of crimes against humanity and corruption.

The Chilean people were victims of the political purge following the violent military overthrow of Salvador Allende (1970–1973), the freely elected Marxist President, a shattering coup engineered by the CIA and rightist Chilean military, which former Secretary of State Colin Powell has called "one of the darker chapters in our history."

Bachelet came from a military family and also received some armed forces administrative training in the United States, and thus became the first woman Minister of Defense in Chilean history. The left-center coalition of Socialists and Christian Democrats who gave her that post has governed Chile after Pinochet relinquished power in 1990. In a compromise between Allende and Pinochet, Chile since then has followed a free-market program with a substantial portion of economic growth channeled into social reforms.

105

It took political savvy and a genuine goal of reconciliation for Bachelet to restore respect by the Chilean people for their military after the Pinochet era, which saw the clandestine deaths of some 2,000 opponents. After the coup of 1973, ending the Popular Unity government of Allende, Bachelet and her mother themselves were held for three weeks in one of the detention camps scattered throughout the country, before being forced into exile in Australia and later East Germany. Press accounts said she was "tortured" but Bachelet herself said later she had been "mistreated." Her father, an Air Force general in the Allende government, was tortured for months before dying of a heart attack in one of the detention centers, which ranged from the desert north to an Antarctic island in this shoestring republic wedged between the Andes and the Pacific.

Thus, in 2006, Michelle Bachelet became the first woman in the Americas to be elected President on her own merits. Although the cult of masculinity in Latin America (*machismo*) has sometimes been exaggerated, women in Chile have had to fight their way to the top. Bachelet appealed to women voters, who comprised only 36 percent of the work force, the lowest percentage in Latin America, according to the *Washington Post* (December 10, 2005). Moreover, women who have jobs make 30 to 40 percent less than their male counterparts. Thus, Bachelet's campaign slogan was directed to these women, "I am with you!" and enlightened males. She also promised that women would fill half of her cabinet positions.

"This isn't the first time, or the last, that Chileans are startling the world," Bachelet said in her inaugural speech. A biographer called her election "the triumph of history defeated." As the new President herself said, as quoted in the *New York Times*, "Violence ravaged my life. I was a victim of hatred, and I have dedicated my life to reversing that hatred . . . I have tried to channel that pain into a constructive realm [what she calls "social inclusion"]. I insist on the idea that what we lived here in Chile was so painful, so terrible, that I wouldn't wish for anyone to live through our situation again."

Some Chileans tried to minimize the significance of Bachelet's election, such as Rafael Gumucio, a writer for *The Clinic* of Santiago, whose article printed in the *New York Times* (December 9, 2005) began: "Chile is one of the more conservative countries on a continent that is not especially renowned as tolerant, forward thinking or democratically minded." On the contrary, before the intervention by the rightist military and the CIA in 1973, Chile was one of the most sophisticated and stable democracies in the hemisphere.

Does Gumucio, author of the article, not know that British Labor leaders went to Chile after World War II to study its national health plan before launching their own? Does he not know that Chile's mixed private and governmental pension system, whatever flaws may have accrued since its inception twenty-five years ago, has been copied by scores of other countries?

And how does he explain the adherence to Constitutional law under extreme pressure when Congress made the final decision, with the grudging support of the Christian Democrats, that put a Marxist candidate, Salvador Allende, in the presidency? After all, his plurality in the election of 1970, but not the required majority, placed the decision up to Congress, according to the Constitution, Allende did receive more votes than any other candidate in the election, and thus Congress bowed to the will of the people.

With my experience in Chile dating back to 1962, I was not in the least surprised at the election of Bachelet as the latest manifestation of the resilience and innovative genius of the Chilean people. Now that Pinochet is gone, Chile has once again become a vibrant democracy where there is a place for all political views.

As an example of Chilean tolerance and pluralism, huge crowds lined the streets in March 2005 to pay homage as the cortege passed by of Gladys Marin, 63, longtime leader of the Chilean Communist Party, who ran for President in 1993 and 1999, and was revered as a champion of women's rights. The government declared two days of national mourning for the passing of this remarkable woman, who was elected to Congress at the age of 24.

Before the turmoil of the Allende years and repression of the Pinochet years, American tourists seemed surprised to see the Chilean Communist Party compete openly and freely with all others in the political spectrum, since the Communist Party had been outlawed in the United States in 1954.

Every Sunday one could see small groups of Chilean Communists parading in orderly fashion quietly down the Alameda, the main thoroughfare of Santiago, whole families in their Sunday best with women holding aloft banners they had made with exquisite needlework. There was no pushing or shoving from bystanders, no cat-calls, and no chanting of stale slogans from the marchers. Most importantly, there were no Carabineros or national policemen in sight. The marchers were just Chileans quietly expressing their political views. It was if they were going to church.

It was my great good fortune to live a year in Santiago and get to know Chileans before their country became a battlefield of conflicting ideologies in the Cold War, exploiting fears at home and abroad which had no relevance to Chile or the United States. The policy to destroy the legitimate government of Chile succeeded only in clamping on the Chilean people seventeen years of one of the harshest dictatorships in Latin America, as we had done earlier in the Caribbean and Central America. But let us begin with my arrival in Chile in 1962.

LIFE BEFORE ALLENDE AND PINOCHET

When we deplaned at the Pudahuel airport some miles from Santiago, the man beside me in a dark blue business suit, perhaps comfortable in the summer of the northern hemisphere which we had just left, took a deep breath of the crisp Chilean winter air of the southern hemisphere, scanned the snow-topped Andes range of mountains, a magnificent backdrop to the cosmopolitan city below, and said, "Well. This isn't so bad!" On the contrary, it was quite good for me, with a freshly minted Ph.D. in history from the University of Virginia under one arm, and a year-long Doherty Foundation grant under the other, ready to embark upon a great adventure.

The first thing to do was find a play to stay. This turned out to be a little apartment in a high-rise building overlooking the busy Alameda. My building had an arcade of shops below and offices above, with small apartments interlaced throughout, some perhaps rented by Chilean businessmen for their mistresses or as places of assignation.

At least, I had an address and quickly learned the custom that one had to tip the mailman, or you wouldn't get any mail. And if you were not home, he would make a mark on the wall near your front door, apprising you of your arrears, after slipping your mail under the door. When I was not at the National Library half a block away, a massive building like a bookend to the massive Union Club at the other end of the Alameda, both aristocratic monuments of another era, I could see from my window the busy daily life of Santiago, such as the country woman sitting on the sidewalk on the corner, hugging her shawl in the winter chill and selling oranges arranged in neat little pyramids.

The owner of my apartment, a matronly and fashionably dressed woman from one of the more affluent suburbs of Santiago, showed up each week to clean the place. This puzzled me until I realized she had an unmarried daughter. I turned for advice to my friend, Rolando Mellafe, now one of Chile's leading historians, who dragooned me every Thursday for lunch at the restaurant Waldorf (yes, Waldorf) to practice his English, without giving a thought to my wanting to polish my Spanish. "The owner cleaning your apartment?" he shouted. In class-conscious Chile, Rolando was aghast. "This could be a tremendous problem," he warned me, but as things turned out, when I offered no signs of encouragement, the landlady finally ceased and desisted, and I did my own cleaning.

Did I mention that her daughter was studying ballet? This is the national passion of Chile, next, of course, to *futbol* (soccer). Bud Wilkinson, when coach of the University of Oklahoma football team, once had his players learn basic ballet, which of course requires more muscular coordination and skill than any sport. As a vignette of Chilean respect for the arts, one Sunday afternoon, I was sitting on a park bench watching a young man practicing his ballet movements. He was good. A bunch of boys playing soccer nearby, noticed him and gathered around to watch. And when he had finished, the soccer boys applauded and then went back to their game.

Speaking of sports, there are no bullfights in Chile—or in numerous other Latin American countries. One can almost feel a shudder run through the audience in a Santiago movie house whenever newsreels from Spain show bullfights. Downtown streets are walkways with benches where people sit and talk. One night, I was sitting on one of those benches watching the world go by. A boy about eight years old, a ragamuffin if I ever saw one, saw me sitting alone and came over to keep me company. In the midst of our conversation, a band of Hare Krishnas trouped by, chanting endlessly. "Why don't they do something useful?" I asked my young companion. "On no, Señor!" he replied. "It is a religion." I learned something that night.

About the Chilean National Library, I soon found it was not easy to get to its enormous treasures. One had to win the good graces of the director, then the elderly Guillermo Feliú Cruz, who guarded his domain as if it were the cornerstone of Western Civilization. (In general, librarians and archivists in Latin America tend to have the maddening idea that their job is to preserve books, not let them be used.)

Before I could tap the Chilean National Library's resources, however, I had to submit to the director an outline and bibliography of what I intended to do—like a schoolboy. After two or three attempts (Feliú Cruz did not understand social history), I was assigned a stool in the basement under a naked light bulb that kept swaying back and forth, and they brought me the bound newspapers. This setting, as I wrote a friend, made me feel like Bob Cratchet, but soon I was promoted to the main reading room, where I could ponder the Chilean past in comfort.

Nevertheless, all of the scholarly sweat in the world could not save Chile from the Juggernaut to come. Henry Kissinger, then national security advisor, in his memoir, *The White House Years*, (1979) recalled that the Group of 40, established in the United States to deal with what was perceived as the threat of an Allende government, abandoned Track I, what they called "the Rube Goldberg gambit," by which Jorge Alessandri, then President, would resign before the final presidential decision by Congress so that Eduardo Frei, leader of the Christian Democrats, would be constitutionally free to run again in an immediate special election.

More serious was Track II, by which the CIA planned the assassination of General René Schneider to ignite a "preventive coup" to block Allende's selection. General Schneider believed in democracy and had pledged the military to abide by the decision of Congress. But his murder, the first of a high Chilean official in 140 years, backfired, stiffening resistance in the Chilean Congress to make their own choice. Edward M. Korry, then U.S. ambassador to Chile, denied before the Church Committee in 1975 (see below) that he, and the Secretaries of State and Defense, did not know of the plan to assassinate General Schneider, set up by the CIA and carried out by Chilean soldiers.

After Allende took office in 1970, every propaganda device possible was used by the right, abetted by the CIA, in an all-out effort to discredit and destroy his administration. This included the celebrated March of the Pots and Pans. Food shortages did develop, resulting in long lines of irate housewives, caused partly by two lengthy strikes by truckers delivering food to Santiago, said to be instigated by the CIA, and the hoarding of food by rightwing distributors.

But the March of the Pots and Pans, in which thousands of women took to the streets banging their empty pans to dramatize the food shortage, was in one sense a hoax. Depicted in the world press as a spontaneous demonstration, it was actually a staged propaganda event whipped up in advance. Rightwing newspapers, which accounted for 80 percent of the national press circulation, urged women three or four days before the event to pour into the streets on the appointed day, assuring a large turn-out and giving international television crews exactly what they wanted.

One newspaper photograph of a "housewife," for example, showed a woman wearing a mink stole and waving aloft a shiny new pan, probably bought for the occasion, and who probably never saw the inside of a kitchen. This, of course, was certainly not representative, but it does indicate the tenor of the occasion.

THE EDWARDS DYNASTY

El Mercurio, Chile's leading newspaper which led the fray of the March of Pots and Pans, was founded 1827 at Valparaíso on the seacoast and bought by the Agustín Edwards family in 1879, who later launched a Santiago edition in 1902. (It was not included in the 40 profiles of *The Elite Press, Great Newspapers of the World* by John Merrill, 1968.) Tomás P. MacHale, a member of the editorial staff of *El Mercurio*, noted that during the political campaign of 1970, "His [Allende's] principal target was 'El Mercurio,' which was rudely attacked before vast audiences." The newspaper supported the conservative Jorge Alessandri, the bachelor President, a tall silver-haired man who used to walk from La Moneda, seat of the executive offices, to his apartment a few blocks away, unescorted before violence came to Chile.

Allende once called *El Mercurio* "that Yankee newspaper in Spanish," but an aide said he read it every morning. The Agustín Edwards family, in its sixth generation at the time of Allende, also owned a ten-newspaper chain in the north of Chile, radio and television stations, and other business enterprises. Their only real competitor was a five-newspaper chain (SOPESUR) owned by the Christian Democrats in the south. The major means of communication was radio, but because of poverty and illiteracy, which hindered the political participation of Chileans living in the countryside, the CIA apparently did not deem it worthwhile to spread propaganda by radio but instead concentrated its efforts on the print medium in the cities.

When Allende's election was imminent in Congress, Agustín Edwards Eastman made a desperate trip to Washington, DC to seek aid from Henry Kissinger, who recalled in his memoir *The White House Years* (1979), "By then [September 14, 1970] Nixon had taken a personal role. He had been triggered into action by Augustin [sic] Edwards, the publisher of the most respected Chilean daily newspaper, who had come to Washington to warn of the consequences of an Allende takeover."

In all, ten million dollars were appropriated, first to block the election of Allende, and then to undermine his government. To some observers, this may not seem like much, but in the precarious balance of power in Chile at the time it was significant.

When Allende was in fact elected by Congress, many business executives and others fled Chile, liquidating what they could of their holdings. Agustín Edwards Eastman, the emissary to Washington and kingpin of the family, stayed in the United States and became a vice-president of Pepsi Cola. His brother Roberto, who had headed Editorial Lord Cochrane and created the women's magazine *Paula*, fled to Argentina.

But Sonia Edwards, also a member of the board of directors of *El Mercurio*, unlike her brothers, stayed in Chile and supported Allende's Popular Unity government. However, she had little or no influence on the newspaper's policy since her brother Agustín Edwards Eastman, who controlled the majority of shares in the *El Mercurio* enterprises, had left his man Arturo Fontaine, a vehement opponent of Allende, in charge.

Sonia Edwards, a psychologist and mother of three children, headed the pro-Allende committee at *El Mercurio*, one of such groups established in many factories and other workplaces. The committee at *El Mercurio* numbered about 100 workers among some 600 altogether. They tried to scrape together enough money to buy a controlling interest in *El Mercurio* itself in order to support Allende, but failed to do so.

Finally, Sonia Edwards was quoted by *Punto Final* (September 28, 1971) as saying, "The possibility of producing a change in the newspaper [*El*

Mercurio] now seems remote to me. *El Mercurio* boycotts the Labor of the Government daily, lies and encourages seditious activities. Therefore, I see that the only solution is expropriation [of a firm she partly owned], so that it passes directly to all the workers."

As opposition against the Allende government increased and life became more difficult in Santiago, the war of words escalated (Allende allowed complete freedom of the press with the two exceptions listed below), into what Chileans called "guerilla journalism." Most virulent among the opposition papers were two publications, *PEC* and *Sepa* which ran such headlines as CHILE IN THE HANDS OF MADMEN and ALLENDE SHOULD BE IMPRISONED. Some Chileans interviewed believed the two publications were founded and financed by the CIA since there were no advertisements or other means of support. In an interview, editor Jaime Valdes said, "It wouldn't have bothered me if the CIA had financed both *PEC* and *Sepa*, but I did not see the money." At any rate, both publications closed up shop immediately after the coup of 1973.

These two newspapers, while the most extreme, were not isolated examples of the attacks on the Allende government. Early on, journalism spun out of control, on both right and left, what one observer called "trench warfare" leading at times to violence in the streets. If one reads the files of *El Mercurio* during the Allende period, it is transparent that the newspaper twisted the news, magnifying everything that went wrong, and exacerbating—or even inventing—clashes between the government and its opponents.

THE ALLENDE GOVERNMENT

Few readers or viewers in the United States probably knew that Salvador Allende was a physician. Nor did they seem to know the difference between Marxism, which in Chile meant peaceful change, what Allende called *La Vía Chilena* (The Chilean Way), and Leninism which advocated violent, revolutionary change. And Americans knew little or practically nothing about the man himself. In every news report, he was always "the Marxist candidate" or "the Marxist President." There was little or no information about what he was trying to accomplish in Chile.

Allende was born in 1908, the son of a lawyer and notary public, and a mother of French descent. He completed his medical training at the University of Chile and served as Minister of Health before deciding to devote himself full-time to politics. Far-reaching public health measures, along with other reforms, could be effected, he thought, only through the national political process. As he once observed, "You can't impose democracy on empty stomachs."

Thus, he ran for the presidency four times, gaining ground with each election (he was 62 when he became President) but he became a standing joke to some. After the third try, for example, *Topaze*, Chile's famous humor magazine, ran a cartoon of a tombstone with the epitaph, "Here lies Salvador Allende, Future President of Chile."

After the election of 1970, *El Mercurio* sent cables throughout the hemisphere warning that it was in imminent danger of being nationalized. The Inter-American Press Association (IAPA), composed mainly of newspaper publishers, adopted a proposal by Lee Hills, president of the Knight newspaper chain, at the meeting of IAPA in Mexico City in 1970, to send a delegation to Chile to determine if freedom of the press were endangered there. Some Chileans resented this intrusion into their affairs, and regarded it as an insult to their long-standing respect for the rule of law. Even *El Mercurio* objected, noting that Chilean journalists would be in a better position to evaluate press freedom there than foreign observers.

Matters worsened a year later when Andrew Heiskel, president of *Time*, cut off a speech by Francisco Galdames, editor of the Socialist *Noticias de Ultima Hora*, who walked out of the Chicago meeting, followed by the entire Chilean delegation. Allende leaped into the fray, expressing the "personal and national hope that *El Mercurio* stops being only the outpost to defend the interests of one of the most powerful clans of Chile and converts itself into a newspaper that defends for once the interests of Chile and the Chileans."

Before the final Congressional election of Allende, the Christian Democrats insisted that freedom of the press and other civil liberties be guaranteed by placing the means of mass communication off limits to expropriation. This was the price of their support for Allende (which to some seemed redundant since these guarantees already were in the Constitution of 1925). Allende also made it clear that of the 30,500 enterprises in Chile, his government would expropriate only the 150 largest, with compensation.

On another front, the Allende forces faced the possible curtailment of newsprint by the opposition. While Juan Domingo Perón had used the meat cleaver approach in cutting off all supplies of newsprint to *La Prensa* and ultimately confiscating the newspaper in 1951, the Allende government sought to get supporters to buy into the two private companies which have always produced all of Chile's paper needs—Compañia Manufactera de Papeles y Cartones (better known as Papelera and owned by President Jorge Alessandri), and Indústrias Forestales. The effort failed miserably, however. Buyers bought only 5.5 percent of the 145 million shares.

In summary, what did the Allende government actually accomplish over-all before being overthrown on September 11, 1973 by the military and CIA? It is difficult to tell, as statistics for this period are unreliable, but changes were clearly underway. The following figures presented in the government newspaper *La Nación* (November 3, 1971) were undoubtedly inflated, but it maintained the Allende administration in its first year had distributed 48 million kilos of powdered milk to four million children, along with massive vaccinations, and had built 75,000 new housing units. Some 1,382 *fundos* or large estates totaling 2,400,000 hectares (a hectare is 2.47 acres) had been redistributed to the previously landless. It must be pointed out, however, that more land and factories were seized and occupied illegally, with no records kept of such actions.

THE CHURCH COMMITTEE REPORT

In the six-week interim between Allende's plurality and his election by Congress, the Senate committee headed by Frank Church (D-Idaho) in 1975 found that the still influential but faltering *El Mercurio* received $1,665,000 from the CIA to keep it afloat and disseminate propaganda.

The Church Committee also found that more than half of the eight million dollars expended by the CIA in Chile between 1963 and 1973 went to righ-twing media and concluded, "The most extensive covert action in Chile was propaganda. It was relatively cheap."

El Mercurio has repeatedly denied taking money from the CIA, filling one whole page on one occasion in an attempt to refute the Church Com-mittee's findings. Two attempts by the author to interview Arturo Fontaine, then in charge of *El Mercurio*, were rebuffed, but a middle-level manager, who asked not to be named, said the money probably went to individual "assets" or bribed journalists on the staff to use or rewrite material supplied by the CIA.

The Church report also indicated that 726 articles, broadcasts and editorials against Allende were placed in the Latin American and European media, in the time between Allende's plurality and congressional election. The Church Committee found "A CIA project renewal memorandum [which] concluded that *El Mercurio* and other media outlets supported by the Agency [the CIA] had played an important role in setting the stage for the September 11, 1973 military coup which overthrew Allende. Freedom of the press was the single most important theme in the international propaganda campaign [against Allende]." The most chilling effect in reading the Church report is that CIA officials who testified before the Committee seemed proud of their work in overthrowing the constitutionally elected government of Chile. Nathaniel Davis, U.S. ambassador to Chile from 1971 until shortly after the 1973 coup, wrote in the *Washington Post*, "For what my own personal testimony is worth, the Church Committee found the truth."

Was freedom of the press threatened during the Allende administration? Only two newspapers—*El Mercurio* and *La Tercera de la Hora*—were closed for a maximum of six days, according to law. The charge against *El Mercurio* was printing an advertisement by the extreme rightwing National Party calling openly for the overthrow of the Allende government. But Allende bowed to a court decision, and lifted restrictions against both newspapers after they had been closed for one day.

THE PINOCHET YEARS

After three years of social unrest, fueled by *El Mercurio*, the CIA and others, residents of Santiago awoke to the news on the radio early on the morning of September 11, 1973, "The press, radio stations and television channels must suspend their informative activities from this moment on, otherwise they will be bombarded from the air and ground."

Thus began the Chilean nightmare that was to last seventeen years under General Augusto Pinochet (1973–1990) which brooked no opposition in one of the most severe backlashes against reform in Latin American history, with some 2,000 political opponents "disappeared" and presumed dead. They were detained without cause or defense, and held incommunicado in prison camps to suffer their fates, which usually ended with torture and death.

Let it be said, however, that these human rights abuses, or crimes against humanity, were less in Chile than neighboring Argentina, where the "dirty war," a phrase coined by the ruling military there itself, sanctioned any means to eliminate political opponents. The tenor of this state terrorism was illustrated by the Argentine General Ibérico Saint-Jean on May 26, 1979, in response to the urban guerrilla warfare of earlier years, "First we will kill all of the subversives, then . . . we will kill their sympathizers, then . . . those who remain undecided, and finally, we will kill the indifferent ones."

But it was not the Organization of American States, which sent an investigating commission, nor Amnesty International or Americas Watch—whose work nevertheless was valuable—that was decisive in revealing to the world the political genocide that was happening in Argentina. It was the Mothers of the Plaza de Mayo (the military called them "the Mad Women of the Plaza de Mayo") whose children or other victims had "disappeared" since the military seized power in 1976.

Every Thursday afternoon (as I have seen), the Mothers of the Plaza de Mayo walked silently in protest in a circle in front of the Casa Rosada, the executive seat of government for years, before finally capturing the attention of the international news media. They are still walking (2008) until every human being is accounted for of the 20,000 to 30,000 "disappeared" during this reign of military state terrorism.

In Chile, events were more sudden and dramatic. The whole world watched by television the aerial bombardment of La Moneda, the massive and imposing seat of the Chilean government in downtown Santiago, and strafing of shantytowns. Allende was almost alone in La Moneda when the Chilean military struck on September 11, 1973, and he apparently committed suicide in the face of troops advancing on the building, although some Chileans believe he was murdered by them.

Initial news reports of this violent attack upon the legitimate government of Chile indicated that civilian casualties were light, but John Barnes of *Newsweek* won the 1973 prize of the Latin American Studies Association for the best U.S. news reporting of that year, proving that civilian casualties were heavy by actually counting bodies in the city morgue and extrapolating from that base.

With the military in power, radios were silenced indefinitely, and military rectors took over the four universities, which operated the four television channels. Prior censorship of all media lasted seven months with military officers actually in the newsrooms approving every item that went into print or on the air.

The close support of *El Mercurio* with the Military Junta which followed the coup of 1973 was evident when the Edwards newspaper was allowed to publish again after ten days, although *Las Ultimas Noticias* and *La Segunda* had to wait four months. Also, the linkage became apparent when Fernando Leniz, highest executive of the Edwards enterprises, was named the second civilian member of the ruling Military Junta, before Pinochet assumed full command.

The press of the left, such as *El Siglo*, voice of the Chilean Communist Party, was completely wiped out, and the spurious Constitution of 1980 (dictators like to legitimize their rule) provided that any journalist even mentioning "class struggle" could get ten years in prison. A new government agency, DINACOS, closely regulated the remainder of Chilean journalism. One had to get permission from this office to start any new publication. Emilio Filippi, one of Chile's most distinguished journalists, had to wait three years to start a mildly adversarial newspaper, *La Epoca*.

Meanwhile, five little magazines opposing Pinochet popped up all over the place, along with everyone's favorite, the little newspaper *Fortín Mapocho*. Censorship and closures, with editors frequently jailed and abused, abounded.

The little satirical magazine, *Bicicleta* (Bicycle), with typical Chilean humor, always carried this notice (in very small print) in every issue they managed to get out:

> The editor does not necessarily share the opinions of the assistant editor, nor vice versa, the three the opinions of other editors, secretaries, printers, artists or managers, nor all of these, the former, because here we all think differently. But not necessarily.

As for the Chilean Catholic Church, contrary to the *New York Times* guest columnist Rafael Gumucio's statement, some segments of the Church opposed the Pinochet regime with vigor and courage. The Jesuit publication *Mensaje* (Message), for example, was the first to uncover the detention camps and to denounce the breakdown of law there with torture and denial of counsel or contact with anyone. Renato Hevia, S.J. was not alone when he revealed other human rights abuses of the Pinochet regime. For his efforts to restore justice, Father Hevia was imprisoned for fifteen days.

Another Church publication, officially sanctioned unlike the Jesuit *Mensaje*, was *Solidaridad*, published by the Vicariate of Solidarity, the social action arm of the Chilean Catholic Church, which found jobs for political outcasts and performed other social services for the afflicted. Pinochet officials prohibited its being sent through the mails, but one could buy a copy at the Vicariate's office next to the National Cathedral on the Plaza de Armas. A small shop tucked away from the street in the Vicariate also offered for sale handicrafts made by political prisoners, each bearing the proud insignia PP (Prisionero Político).

Somewhere along the line, I hooked up with a savvy young man, Patricio Corvalán Estefanía, who for many summers (their winters) opened doors for me closed to newsmen breezing through. A sidekick, amanuensis, chief bottle washer, and one who was street wise, like all Chileans at times he could not restrain himself. Once, in a small cafe with nearby couples talking in subdued tones, we were quietly discussing Pinochet when Patricio suddenly blurted out, in a loud voice, "Why don't they kill him?" I wanted to slide under the table.

As a young soldier several years earlier, Patricio had witnessed one of the executions of political dissidents and their burial in a mass grave. He was born into a poor mining camp family in the north of Chile where there was no school. When his family later moved to Santiago in search of work, he began the first grade as an adolescent. Because of his age, his classmates mocked him, calling him "*tonto!*" (Fool!) but he breezed through grade school in a couple of years and let it go at that.

When it came time for me to leave Santiago—for the last time—with the civilian government of Patricio Aylwyn in place, and I had received the

Freedom Forum award of the Gannett Foundation for my long-term coverage of the Pinochet dictatorship, Patricio and I were strolling quietly through an open-air marketplace, not saying much, when he stopped at one of the stalls which sold little black pottery pigs, and bought one to give me.

All of them had only three legs, the trademark of the craftsmen of the province of Chillán who made them, and they were supposed to bring you good luck. Patricio told me the story behind those little black pigs. It seems one of them wanted his mother to explain why he had only three legs, and at first she said it was because they came from a very poor family and there simply were not enough legs to go around. Not satisfied, the son pressed on, and his mother finally replied, "Look, it is not important how many legs you have. It's what you do with those you do have that counts."

But my life centered on San Diego street, the Greenwich Village of Chile, and Luis Rivano who loved books. He almost hated to part with them when he sold any, and I once saw a look of sorrow come over his face when he was examining a rare book and saw that the spine had been slightly torn. He was a former Carabinero or national policeman, a corps established in the 1920s to counter-balance the regular army. Carabineros were known throughout Chile for their brown uniforms and close relations with the Chilean people. Before the Pinochet regime brutalized them, the Carabineros were regarded by many Chileans with the same affection and respect the British once showed their Bobbies.

The Carabineros took on the project in 1962 to clean up the neglected grave of poet Gabriela Mistral, the first Latin American winner of the Nobel Prize for literature, to be followed by Pablo Neruda in 1970, making Chile the only Latin American country to boast two Nobel laureates in literature. Before being awarded the Prize, Neruda—an active member in the Chilean Communist Party—was in a Santiago cafe when a Chilean reporter approached him and asked, "Sr. Neruda, if you, seated here at this table, would be offered either the presidency of Chile or the Nobel Prize, what would you do?" Without hesitation, Neruda replied, "I would move to another table."

As a footnote to history, Neruda died within days after the coup of 1973. Suffering from cancer, he was taken to a clinic in Santiago from his seaside home, Isla Negra, later ransacked by Chilean soldiers, who also destroyed priceless manuscripts. Upon his death, 20,000 Chileans defied a curfew to accompany him on his cortege to the city's central cemetery. The only notice in *El Mercurio's* obituary section was "Died. In Santiago. Pablo Neruda. Poet."

Years later, I decided to visit the grave of Pablo Neruda. Wandering around the central cemetery looking for it, I asked an ancient woman cooking some food over a small fire, clearly a permanent resident of the cemetery, "Where is the grave of Pablo Neruda?" She cackled, "It's next to the one reserved for Pinochet!" Although I expected some ornate monument, I found instead a

simple crypt with only the name Pablo Neruda on the front, about three feet
by three feet, where those who had come to pay their respects had written little messages. The one I remember most was, "Pablo, you are still with us."

Paco (Chilean slang for cop), as Luis Rivano was called, advanced the arts
among his fellow Carabineros by hustling books for their library and even
publishing a little mimeographed *Hojas de Poesía* (Leaves of Poetry). Paco
knew everyone who was anyone on the Chilean literary scene and twisted
the arms of some of Chile's leading poets for original contributions. No one
could resist Paco.

But Luis Rivano ran into trouble with his literary ambitions. After eleven
years of service in the Carabineros, he was booted out in 1964 for writing
a socially realistic novel about the Corps, *Esto no es el Paraíso* (This Isn't
Paradise). Zig-Zag, the leading Chilean publisher, was going to publish the
novel, but a police official demanded to see the manuscript and then ordered
Paco to modify it. Luis Rivano refused, and Zig-Zag, later expropriated by
the Allende government, backed out.

The book, published by Rivano himself with the help of friends, was phe-
nomenally successful. It launched him on a career which one critic called "the
most spectacular within this generation." The first press run of 1,000 copies
(there are limited markets for books in much of Latin America because of illiteracy and poverty) sold out in 15 days, and six more printings brought the
total to 12,000.

For his literary efforts, Luis Rivano was booted out of the Carabineros.
There he was at the age of 46, a cop with no job, living in one room with his
wife and four children, and selling books out of a suitcase on the sidewalk.
By the time I knew him, however, he had built up a prosperous bookshop
with several branches and dabbled in dramaturgy. *This Isn't Paradise* could
not be adapted for the theater, however, because the Pinochet regime forbade
the depiction of any uniformed characters on stage. Once, when the Pan-
American games were underway in Santiago, Paco and I were walking down
the Alameda and several tall athletes, obviously from the United States, were
ahead of us, towering above the crowd. "See that?" Paco asked. "That's why
we dislike you."

Whenever I arrived in Santiago, I always headed first for San Diego street
and my friend Luis Rivano, not only to greet him, but to find out what was
going on. Once he asked me, with a puzzled look on his face, "Why do you
do this? Why do you spend miserable winters here when you could be enjoy-
ing summers in Europe?" At that very moment, a Carabinero, despised at
that time (there was even talk of changing their uniforms once Pinochet was
gone) came in and stood there and gazed wistfully at the shelves and shelves
of books while Luis Rivano greeted him warmly. And therein lay the answer
to Paco's question.

Chapter Six

The Sandinista Revolution in Nicaragua and the Chamorro Family

Victor Andrade, a Bolivian diplomat whose opinion I valued, once said that Americans needed some preventive education before going abroad. From the publication of *The Ugly American* by William K. Lederer and Eugene Burdick in 1958 to the present, to many we seem like adolescents wanting the rest of the world to like us and wondering why they don't.

A recent travel article in the *Washington Post* (August 12, 2007) by John Briley, perhaps free-lance, stated, "When I first heard `Nicaragua' and `tourism' in the same sentence four years ago, I pictured a lawless country, bombed-out roads, bandits and a gastrointestinal hit job." While Mr. Briley did not intend to write a political piece, he described Daniel Ortega as "loosely-hinged." He was the leader of the Frente Sandinista of National Liberation (FSLN) which successfully vanquished the entrenched dictatorship of Anastasio Somoza Debayle in 1979, and had just been elected President of Nicaragua after gracefully accepting defeat in two previous free and open elections.

But there was more to this little travel article than the passing reference to Ortega, which revealed the lack of knowledge of many about the history and culture of Nicaragua. The author was scouting for cheap real estate for retired Americans springing up everywhere, especially in Mexico and Central America. These enclaves are made up of residents who cluster together without making any effort to understand or mingle with the society of their host countries. They may contribute somewhat to the local economy, but few make any attempt to learn Spanish, except to order their servants around.

The travel writer found in Nicaragua only what he expected to find, noting, "Driving out of Managua in late May (2007), I saw a weary country. The six-month dry season had rendered the land brown and dusty. Emaciated livestock picked at shriveled weeds, shanties dotted the roadside, and desperate residents shoveled dirt into potholes, then stuck their hands out to passing cars. That Third World smell—high particulate exhaust blended with garbage and a whiff of sewage—sullied the air."

The civil war in Nicaragua had been complicated for the Sandinistas once in power by the illegally funded "contras" or counter-revolutionaries organized by the American military officer Oliver North. Nicaraguans claim his surreptitious trading of hostages for arms from Iran only added another 50,000 victims to the casualty list of the 25,000 killed in the struggle against Somoza. North became a tabloid hero in the United States. When he appeared in full military dress uniform at the subsequent Congressional hearings, with a chestful of medals, one observer likened his hangdog look as that somewhere between Gary Cooper and Huckleberry Finn.

When the Sandinistas were victorious in July 1979 after a nineteenth-month conflict that cost a total of 45,000 lives, according to the Red Cross estimate, they faced the ruins of a country that had been bled dry by the Somoza family, which owned about three-fourths of the land and controlled business, especially banking. Their estate was estimated in uninflated terms at $500 million dollars, a staggering sum for a small country the size of Connecticut.

The Sandinistas also inherited the emotional baggage of intermittent rule by United States Marines between 1909 and 1933, establishing and leaving behind the National Guard to maintain order. Within a year, however, Anastasio Somoza Garcia, founder of the dynasty, had gained control of the National Guard and, from his viewpoint, used it effectively as his vehicle to gain and maintain power until his assassination in 1956. His son, Anastasio Somoza Debayle, with several front-men interludes—ruled until being overthrown by the Sandinistas in 1979, when he and his entourage fled to Miami—taking the family remains with them—and finally finding refuge in the dictatorial regime of General Alfredo Stroessner in Paraguay.

There were debts to be settled in Nicaragua, however. In December 1979, the Junta of National Reconstruction set up nine tribunals to judge some 4,500 former National Guardsmen on charges of murder, and 2,500 more Somoza collaborators accused of fraud, theft, torture, extortion and other crimes. Somoza himself was tried for genocide in absentia since Paraguay had no extradition treaty with Nicaragua. The others, each provided with counsel, faced no more than 30 years in prison, because Nicaragua did not have the death penalty. In charge of the tribunals, with trials expected to last six months, was Nora Astorga, who had the authority to free anyone before they came to trial for insufficient evidence, and welcomed observers from Amnesty International and other human rights groups to witness the proceedings.

The triumph of the Sandinista guerrillas in Nicaragua in 1979 after a nineteen-month battle against the dictatorship of Anastasio Somoza Debayle, who with his family had ruled the country like his fiefdom for forty-three years, inaugurated a new phase in Nicaraguan history.

Upon arriving in Managua shortly after the fighting stopped in July 1979, the first thing that struck me was the devastation caused by the 1972 earthquake that had leveled central Managua, a vast emptiness where only grass grew except for the two-story wooden building in the center of this devastation that housed the Government of National Reconstruction, consisting of five Junta members, two of whom were civilians, all on the second floor in one big room.

Nicaraguans do not forget that Somoza pocketed most of the earthquake relief money which poured into their country from all over the world. They have been rebuilding Managua in a ring around the old city, the epicenter of the 1972 earthquake. At the time of my visit, Nicaragua actually had two governments, the administrative arm mentioned above and the military arm, the *Frente Sandinista de Liberación Nacional* (FSLN, Sandinista Front of National Liberation) which held actual power. The latter, now a legitimate political party, swept all ten municipal elections in 2005, an event which got a minor paragraph in the *New York Times*, and ultimately elected their leader Daniel Ortega to the presidency in 2007. Network television news described Ortega as "a former Communist," but in reality he had accepted defeat in two honest elections after the fighting stopped. A political cartoon in the United States after the first election, showed Daniel Ortega rafting across the Gulf of Mexico to the waiting arms of Fidel Castro who was pictured as exclaiming, "You lost a WHAT?"

When I arrived in Managua in December 1979, I noticed in the taxi on the way to my *pensión* (boarding house) a little pendant which swang back and forth over the dashboard, proclaiming the good news, "Merry Christmas Without Somoza." The *pensión*, run by a German woman, boasted a beer cooler in the lobby and was a subculture in itself. I remember a German woman journalist glued to the television set to pass that filtered news on to her readers or viewers.

Down the littered street a ways was a restaurant where I ate and hobnobbed with the help. The restaurant had been turned over to its workers, and it was fascinating to see them conduct their own business meeting without being told what to do. A young chef with his white uniform and tall chef's hat was perched on top of a tall cabinet, totally absorbed in the proceedings.

At another time, I stood by a small outdoor lunch stand, in a break from my research at the nearby library of the Jesuit University of Central America, where Fernando Cardenal, brother of the poet, was rector before being temporarily suspended from the Jesuit order. Buildings at this University have been renamed for martyred students who died in the struggle against Somoza. At the lunch counter, I watched young men playing baseball in the field below. They were having a great time. "This is what young men should be doing," I thought, "not killing each other."

The human touch, suppressed so long, was evident everywhere in Managua. The Sandinistas brought entertainment to the poor *barrios* or neighborhoods (if they can be called that) where children—who had never even seen television before—watched with wide eyes live magicians and other entertainers provided by the Sandinistas. A woman with a kindly face spotted me in one such crowd and came over, offering me a folding chair, and bringing me a piece of cake. She brought me not only a piece of cake, but a piece of the spirit of the Revolution itself.

When Somoza was still in power, various means of propaganda flooded Managua, as the fighting edged nearer the city. Youngsters would hop on buses, make their short spiel on the aims and goals of the FSLN and then hop off at the next stop before they could be nabbed by the police or National Guard. During periods of censorship, radio announcers would go to the churches (invoking sanctuary) and read the uncensored news from the pulpits during the noon hour, which people called "news of the catacombs." Political graffiti or *pintas* were painted on walls everywhere, (Latin America's more colorful version of billboards) such as this one I saw at the corner of Calle Miguel Mercado: "The sons of Sandino will never sell themselves or surrender. Each house will be a Sandista headquarters. Each place a field of battle. Long live the Sandinista unity!"

Earlier, the headquarters of the FSLN had been hidden in the fastness of Chipote, the mountain whose name was applied later to the fortified bunker of Somoza near the National Palace. During Somoza's tenure, both radio and television were completely controlled, and Somoza owned Channel 6 outright. At that time there were about 50 radio stations in all of the country, 15 in Managua. After 1979 the *Sistema Sandinista de Televisión* sought to influence public opinion, while in radio the *Voz de Nicaragua* presented the civil government's side, and *Radio Sandino* that of the FSLN. The Junta of National Reconstruction had no political structure and little experience in government while the military FSLN held real power.

La Barricada, founded shortly after Managua fell, was the official spokesman of the FSLN, but it also published paragraphs from anyone, "if they are of social interest," according to editor Carlos Fernando Chamorro, then 23 and bursting with revolutionary zeal. On the wall of the small offices which had housed Somoza's *Novedades* was a poster which proclaimed, "It is our revolutionary duty to denounce any vestige of *somocista* influence which may place obstacles in our newspaper's march."

This young editor was the son of Pedro Joaquín Chamorro, editor of *La Prensa*, the major Nicaraguan newspaper, widely known for his struggle for press freedom throughout Latin America, but more importantly for his lifelong battle to return Nicaragua to the Nicaraguans. The years of verbal combat against the Somoza dynasty brought him periodic imprisonment, fines, exile and death threats. His wife Violeta, who became a political figure of stature in her own right, told me, "We received so many death threats that we became accustomed to them."

After gun-running and an abortive "invasion," Pedro Joaquín Chamorro relied on the power of words through the family newspaper *La Prensa*, which became a symbol of resistance against Somoza. He allowed it leeway only to demonstrate that freedom of the press existed in Nicaragua. Even this was curtailed, however, with strict censorship during times of siege, one of which lasted almost three years.

For his incessant attacks on the Somoza dynasty, Chamorro was gunned down while driving to work on January 10, 1978. His widow, Violeta Chamorro, served first on the Junta of National Reconstruction and later was elected President. She is a strikingly handsome woman who did not attempt to hide the anger in her voice when she told me she was convinced that her husband had been killed on the direct orders of Somoza, not by over-zealous partisans, seven of whom were rounded up by accusations that led nowhere. "Not a thing happened in this country, not even to a fly, that Somoza did not know about," Violeta Chamorro said.

The devotion to her husband by some 10,000 Nicaraguans was evident in 1979 when I saw them parade around the plaza named for him on the first anniversary of his death. People from all over the country came to honor him, some carrying flowers, others little native replicas of his likeness. Carlos Fernando Chamorro, the young editor of *La Barricada*, declared in an interview that the murder of his father was the "definitive impulse" which fueled the revolutionary spiral by winning over the middle class in the cities.

Somoza himself did not need newspaper support with the ubiquitous National Guard, and few believed his newspaper, *Novedades,* founded in 1948, which only had a circulation of 8,000.

On the other hand, its mission deemed accomplished, *La Barricada* ceased publication on January 30, 1998 (Adam Jones, *Beyond the Barricades*, 2002) although some observers found its tone too shrill to be effective propaganda, and Daniel Ortega was elected President in 2007 without it. In fact, *La Barricada* tended to alienate the very group of moderates who had tipped the scales against Somoza in 1979. But Carlos Fernando Chamorro, its editor, who had fought at Masaya and Managua, did not realize that his Revolution was over, and the people no longer wanted inflammatory slogans.

The Chamorro family itself, one of the most highly regarded in Nicaragua, was split over the direction the Revolution should take after the military phase ended in 1979. As the FSLN moved more to the left, Violeta Chamorro, widow of the slain editor of *La Prensa*, resigned from the Junta, along with Alfonso Robelo, the millionaire industrialist and the only other civilian member of the Junta, leaving others the staggering task of rebuilding a shattered economy, and many considered his expertise and empathy for social change a great loss.

Xavier Chamorro, brother of the editor who considered the family newspaper "a republic of paper," found the postwar *La Prensa* too adversarial against the new Sandinista government and broke away to found his own newspaper, *El Pueblo* which appeared on March 29, 1979 under the editorship of Melvin Wallace. The average age of the staff, including Wallace, was under 30, and 40 percent worked without pay. It was the first collective newspaper in Nicaraguan press history with a minuscule staff of only nine full-time journalists and seventeen *socios obligados* who did special columns.

Thus, the Chamorro family was split three ways—Violeta holding down the fort at *La Prensa*, which then considered itself a "pluralistic newspaper," Xavier launching a moderate Sandinista newspaper, *El Pueblo*, and Carlos Fernando sticking by his guns at *La Barricada*. Melvin Wallace, editor of the offshoot *El Pueblo*, charged that the FSLN "wants to be the only voice of the left in Nicaragua." It speaks volumes for Nicaraguan culture that despite their political differences, the Chamorro family gathered every evening for a cordial dinner. And for those who saw totalitarianism, whether of right or left, looming on the horizon, almost every political party after Somoza had its own newspaper, such as the irregular *Orientación Popular* put out by the Partido Socialista Nigüerence.

But the person I wanted to see most in Nicaragua was Ernesto Cardenal, the poet-priest influenced by the 1968 Latin American Bishops Conference at Medellín, Colombia. It had been inspired by the Second Vatican Council of 1965, which advocated Church action to alleviate the poor and suffering of the under-developed or non-developed world. The creed of this "liberation theology" was based on the New Testament verse of Matthew 10:34, in which Jesus was quoted as saying, "I came not to bring peace but the sword," to right the wrongs of the world. After two trips to Cuba in 1970 and 1971, Ernesto Cardenal, who had studied literature at Columbia University and was briefly a Trappist monk at Gethsemane, Kentucky, made his reputation with the long epic poem, *Hora Cero* (Zero Hour) about the Nicaraguan national hero Augusto César Sandino, who fought the U.S. Marines who had occupied his country intermittently from 1909 to 1933.

Sandino himself, still fighting in the mountains after the Marines left, was assassinated in 1934, but as the prime national hero, his name was used by the

FSLN, formed by a small group of guerrilla fighters in exile in Honduras in 1961 led by Carlos Fonseca Amador, Tomas Borge and a few others.

I walked up a slight hill, El Retoro, to the building where Ernesto Cardenal, one of the most prominent exponents of liberation theology, held court as Minister of Culture. There I found a flock of young people working diligently, and in their midst was Ernesto Cardenal, in blue jeans, white smock and black beret with flowing white hair and angelic face. He was 55 years old then, since suspended from the Church, and told me he had been converted to the theology of liberation at the age of thirty-one, which justified force to bring about social justice if all other means failed. This man, who had published some thirty works of poetry, said he had supported the FSLN, providing a haven or base for some Sandinistas on his retreat established in 1965 in the Solentiane Islands in the southern end of Lake Nicaragua. But it was not true, he told me, that he had actually fought with arms, as the priest Camilo Torres had done in Colombia earlier before being killed and thrust into martyrdom. Cardenal was forced into exile when Somoza's National Guard destroyed his lay community in 1977, and he served as the FSLN's foreign spokesman during the fighting.

When Pope John Paul II visited post-revolutionary Nicaragua in 1980, he shook an admonishing finger at the kneeling Cardenal, a priest and perhaps the finest Nicaraguan poet since Rubén Dario. The Pope was chastising Cardenal in a publicly humiliating way for embracing liberation theology before and during the Sandinista Revolution (although the Pope later also attacked "savage capitalism.")

Years later, Cardenal was quoted in a rare interview with Juan O. Tamayo of the Knight Ridder News Service (January 24, 1999) as saying, when it appeared that liberation theology was waning, "I am still a revolutionary who defends the poor. But liberation theology is in crisis. Capitalism won. What more can be said?"

The presence of oil on the continental shelf discovered by United States firms off the Atlantic coast of Nicaragua may have partly explained American support of Somoza, according to Nicaraguan expert Luis Pasos Argüello. But Somoza did not have time to exploit it, much as the possibility of a trans-isthmian canal across Nicaragua had aroused interest earlier before Panama was severed from Colombia for the present route.

Immediately after the fighting stopped in Nicaragua in 1979, internal security was deemed a problem. Under the *Comité de Defensa Civil*, which had been formed as early as 1976, every sector of the city had one CDS representative responsible for each block. It was rather disconcerting to see armed *Sandinistas* prowling around in the dark, but they maintained that their job was simply to maintain public order, not attempt any kind of ideological control, as in Cuba.

After the death of Pedro Joaquín Chamorro, control of the family newspaper *La Prensa* temporarily passed to his brother Xavier Chamorro who once said, "*La Prensa* has always had two directors because one or the other was usually in jail." The newspaper felt the wrath of the Somoza dictatorship. On June 11, 1979, the physical plant of *La Prensa* was destroyed when tanks rolled up and National Guardsmen doused gasoline within the building and torched it. The fire lasted two days, but repeated calls for fire engines went unheeded.

La Prensa also witnessed the terrorist tactics of the FSLN, whether the assault on the Christmas party at the home of José María Castillo, a leading *somocista*, on December 26, 1974, a gathering which U.S. Ambassador Turner Catledge had left only twenty minutes earlier, or the more spectacular occupation of the National Palace in 1978, with the taking of some 500 hostages, including twenty-four journalists inside covering proceedings. Television footage showed people jumping out of windows to escape their captors. With the bargaining power of FSLN leader Edén Pastora, ten million dollars in ransom money was paid, FSLN proclamations were printed in all of the newspapers (terrorism would be futile without news media coverage) and the seventeen instigators—with their black and red FSLN scarves—were safely escorted one by one by the Archbishop of Nicaragua, Obando y Bravo, to a waiting plane and exile. Somoza declared a state of siege, and later ordered indiscriminate aerial bombing of cities in the interior.

What did the Sandinista Revolution mean to the man in the street? Jorge Eduardo Martínez, a seventeen-year-old waiter who had fought at the battle of León a year earlier, spoke for others with whom I talked when he declared, "Now the rich cannot look at a person and say he is worth nothing. Now all of us are equal." His friend, Ulíses García Ríos, added his belief that the Revolution was "democratic socialism."

The makeshift government hastily constructed after the Sandinista military victory was both bureaucratic and broke. The Ministry of Culture, for example, had no budget, nor did the other eighteen cabinet members. The Direction of Press and Propaganda reported some 32 separate government agencies from Ministries on down.

Nicaragua lost 20 percent of its production during the conflict, according to government official Julio López. He said that the most pressing needs in his war-torn country—and the basic goals of the FSLN itself—were providing health care, food, work and education for all the people. He realized these goals could not be met immediately, but added, "The people have shown great maturity in knowing that everything cannot be satisfied all at once."

Counter-revolution was also in the air, with the "Freedom Fighters" of Oliver North. In my attempt to enter a building to penetrate the maze of propaganda offices, I was confronted by a young Sandinista, an angel-faced boy sitting in a doorway with a sub-machine gun cradled in his lap, who demanded to see my credentials. Fortunately, I had obtained a Nicaraguan press card bordered with blue and white stripes, the national colors, which seemed to register with the boy, who obviously could not read. To allow him to save face, I waited for him to study the card carefully, and finally he waved me through.

Nicaragua was at the crossroads. In the absence of any discernible Latin American policy in the administration of President George W. Bush, whose five-country tour late in his second term was a disaster, although not quite as bad as the mob assaulting the limousine in which Richard M. Nixon was seated in 1958, pelting it with stones and rocking the vehicle. The days of the Good Neighbor Policy and the Alliance for Progress receded into the dim past.

Thus, Nicaragua looked to other sources for sustenance. When Daniel Ortega, 61, was finally inaugurated President of Nicaragua in 2007, prominent among those honoring him was Hugo Chávez of Venezuela, who promised Nicaragua 32 badly needed electricity plants and low-interest loans to the poor from his petro-dollars. Also present was Evo Morales of Bolivia, whose election Chávez also had supported. The Aymará Indian said, "Daniel Ortega's win gives strength and hope not only to Nicaragua but to all of Latin America." Although Fidel Castro could not attend because of intestinal surgery in July 2007, he sent a letter in which he pledged his "utmost support" for Ortega.

Chávez, by the way, had just been elected President of Venezuela for a six-year term, but his Bolivarian pipedream of a united South America went crashing down. He is best remembered, perhaps, for his clumsy histrionics at the United Nations when he called President Bush "a devil." Those Americans who took umbrage tend to forget that they themselves have never hesitated to refer to Latin Americans as banana republics, greasers, spics, or what have you. Evo Morales of Bolivia played it cool at the United Nations, however, simply holding up a coca leaf and grinning impishly.

Help for Nicaragua came from another, unexpected source when Iran promised to finance a new $350 million ocean port, build 10,000 houses for those who endured in the shantytowns, and a $120 million hydroelectric project. (Ortega had gone to Tehran in June 2007, and President Mahmoud Ahmadinejad returned the visit to Managua in January 2008.) Again, the lack of any coherent Latin American policy by the United States left a vacuum which others were all too anxious to fill.

(Compiled from Jerry W. Knudson, "The Nicaraguan Press and the Sandinista Revolution," *Gazette, The International Journal of Communication Studies*, 27 (1981), 163–179.)

Chapter Seven

The Peruvian Press Law of 1974:
A Glimpse of the Future?

The year 1974 seems a long time ago, but something happened that year in Peru which may affect the Latin American press. A colleague in the Department of Journalism at Temple University, Sidney Head, a specialist in the African press, called my attention to a tiny advertisement in the *New York Times* placed by the reform military government of General Juan Velasco Alvarado, who seized power in Peru in 1968 by ousting elected President Fernando Belaunde Terry. The ad pleaded for understanding of his regime's efforts to restructure Peru's press system, stratified almost since colonial days as an elite press controlled mainly by the famous "40 Families" who held the social and economic reins of power. In the ad, the Peruvian military invited foreign observers to come to Peru and see for themselves the changes taking place in the journalism of their country, amidst a storm of protest from United States publishers against the transition in Peru from a class press to a mass press.

Regardless of its heavy handedness and in some instances squelching of individual opposition, General Juan Velasco Alvarado and his crew represented a new breed of military in Latin America, one which was interested in social reform rather than for its own sake, a technocratic harbinger of things to come. They challenged the power of the traditional civilian rulers of Peru in bold and innovative ways. They thus took a step unprecedented in the history of Latin American journalism by nationalizing the eight Peruvian newspapers of major circulation, with the plan of turning them over to various sectors of society, such as labor, campesinos (Indians), teachers and others to own and operate, each stressing news and opinion relevant to their constituents, with no governmental control once the transition to the sectors was effected. And there was compensation to the former owners, who had never addressed the needs of the vast majority of Peruvians.

Cries of violation of freedom of the press dominated the editorial pages of newspapers in the United States, by writers who had never been to Peru or had never heard of A.J. Liebling's bon mot in the *New Yorker*, "Freedom of the Press belongs to those who can afford one." At any rate, it seemed to me manifestly unfair that those attempting social reforms in Peru could get only a tiny paid paragraph in the *New York Times*, so I packed my bags and left on the next flight to Lima.

There I interviewed in 1976 all Peruvian editors concerned, new and hold-overs, including their substantial views on how the new press law of 1974 was working, along with my own assessment, in the selection which follows. All too often, we do not listen to voices from the Third World, but they may have much to tell us. Readers may judge for themselves the viability or promise of the Peruvian press law of 1974, which never had a chance to get off the ground. Because the Peruvian military proved inept in other areas, particularly economics and finance, they were booted out of power in 1980. The eight national newspapers were returned to their owners, and elections brought the perennial Peruvian politician Fernando Belaunde Terry, who had been deposed by the military in 1968, back to power. To some Peruvians, this turn of events marked the end of a noble experiment.

THE PERUVIAN PRESS LAW OF 1974:
THE OTHER SIDE OF THE COIN

On September 23, 1974, the revolutionary Peruvian regime then headed by General Juan Velasco Alvarado launched a unique experiment in the history of the world press. The ruling military expropriated Peru's five major press enterprises and pledged to turn over the eight newspapers they controlled to various sectors of the population for ownership and direction. In a communique published as an advertisement in the *New York Times*, the Peruvian government asserted that "this is the first time in history that a state has placed the press under direct ownership of the people." Although this may have been the intent of the Velasco regime, the promise had not yet been completely fulfilled.

When the newspaper plants were actually taken over on September 27, 1974, a storm of protest reverberated throughout the Western nations, accustomed as industrialized democracies to a long tradition of press freedom.

Leading the attack was the Inter American Press Association (IAPA), an organization of hemisphere newspaper publishers founded in 1926 and reorganized in 1950. IAPA President Robert U. Brown called the Peruvian action "the blackest day for hemispheric press freedom since Perón confiscated most of the press of Argentina 25 years ago and Castro seized the press of Cuba." Germán E. Ornes, chairman of the IAPA Committee on Freedom of the Press and Information, added that the takeover was "an arrogant abuse of power based mainly on the persuasive use of guns." In the succeeding three years, the organization newsletter, *IAPA News*, commented on the press situation in Peru no less than 19 times.

The *New York Times* and other prominent newspapers have repeatedly editorialized against what were deemed to be violations of freedom of expression in Peru.

The purpose of this paper is to present the Peruvian government's side of this controversy, based mainly on interviews in August 1976 with all the government-appointed editors of the newspapers.

The new press law came after a steadily escalating conflict between Peruvian mass communications and the military junta which gained power in a bloodless coup on October 3, 1968, by ousting elected President Fernando Belaunde Terry. The military men who took over control of the country called themselves populist and technocratic—determined to bring about social and economic reforms similar to those accomplished by Mexico since 1910, Bolivia since 1952 and Cuba since 1959. Their social revolution has been moderate, but it has achieved advances in agrarian reform, regaining control of national resources, and bringing workers into ownership participation in industry. Military infighting placed General Francisco Morales Bermúdez in charge on August 29, 1975, and he has maintained the press law intact, although other societal changes have slowed down.

The eclectic ideology of the Peruvian revolution is described by the state as nationalist and independent, rejecting both the capitalist and communist systems. Its doctrine is called "revolutionary humanism" which "expresses itself essentially in socialist thought, in libertarian thinking and in Christian thought." The key to understanding the Peruvian press law of 1974, however, is the regime's emphasis on what is termed a "participatory state" in which all people are said to have access to power—including the means of mass communication—in a pluralist society.

Worked out specifically in terms of the press law, this meant that all newspapers of national distribution—those with more than 20,000 circulation or which reach more than half of the departmental capitals—were expropriated from their owners and placed at the disposal of societal sectors. The law provided for compensation of 10 percent in cash and the rest in annual installments over a ten-year period with 6 percent interest, but the government has not yet done this. *Expreso* and *Extra*, first nationalized in 1970 and made into cooperatives or "Industrial Communities," were included among the eight newspapers taken over by the government.

Until the sectors could organize themselves, the regime appointed committees, each headed by a director, to manage the affairs of each newspaper.
This was to have been an interim measure, but each year since 1974 on the
anniversary of the press law the government has postponed for another year
sector control of the newspapers. When the transfer is made, it is intended to
work like this: an assembly (asociación civil) elected by sector organizations
will become the owner of the newspaper, name its director, and in turn elect
an executive council (consejo directivo) which will oversee day-to-day operations of the newspaper. This council will be composed of seven members
representing the organized sector and three from the newspaper staff, including the managing director.

The actual assignment of the eight newspapers seems not to have followed
a predetermined pattern. *El Comercio*, the second oldest newspaper in the
Spanish language, founded in 1839 and owned by the Miró Quesada family, went to the *campesinos* or Indian peasants. It caused some amusement
in Lima that the most conservative of the Peruvian newspapers with a long
commercial orientation would go to simple farmers. Nevertheless, weekly
supplements and daily columns are addressed to the *campesino* sector, hoping to help raise their level of literacy and interest them in national affairs. *La
Prensa*, the second major Peruvian newspaper, founded in 1903 and owned
by the Beltrán family, became the spokesman of the labor sector. Other allo-
cations were *Correo* to professional organizations (lawyers, engineers, physi-
cians, economists and the like); *Expreso* and *Extra*, educational organizations
(teachers, students and their parents); *Ojo*, cultural organizations (writers,
artists and intellectuals in general); *Ultima Hora*, service organizations
(construction, banks, commerce, transport and others). *Afición*, the eighth
newspaper, apparently did not survive the reorganization. *La Crónica*, and its
later edition *La Tercera*, had been nationalized earlier to serve as government
spokesmen along with *El Peruano*, the official daily newspaper.

Access to the press was the professed object of this dramatic reshuffling.
As Oscar Faura, head of the press department of the Peruvian Foreign Ministry, declared soon after the event, the expropriated newspapers had largely
reflected the views of the privileged "40 families" who had run Peru since
colonial times, appointing presidents and controlling governments. As the
preamble to the press statute itself explained, "It is indispensable that the
press organs of greatest influence in the formation of the national conscience
stop being spokesmen and defenders of minority interests."

There were other considerations as well, however, and self-defense was
not least among them. Military leaders in Peru had watched Salvador Allende
in Chile be undermined—partly, at least—by a free and licentious press,
whereas Fidel Castro in Cuba was secure in the midst of a social revolution

which had frankly abolished press freedoms. The Peruvian junta was not willing to go that far.

Smaller publications were allowed to continue—although many were closed later—but with strict procedures for rectification or clarification of libels. The press statute also provides that every newspaper must have a letters-to-the-editor section. It is forbidden to publish documents or editorials that prejudice "the security of the State or the national defense." Likewise, it is punishable by one to three years in prison "to threaten injury or in any other manner offend the dignity or decorum of the high dignitaries of State . . ." Another provision of the law, carried over from the 1969 press decree, is that publishers cannot be out of the country more than six months at a time—an effort to cut down on absentee ownership.

Another function of the 1974 press law is that of propaganda. Although the government theoretically will not own the newspapers or appoint their editors in the future, the sector spokesmen are expected to espouse the goals and ideals of the Peruvian revolution. According to the press statute, the revamped newspapers "will constitute authentic channels of expression and diffusion of the distinct ideological focuses encompassed within the parameters of the Peruvian Revolution." But this is to be a two-way street. As Article 24 spells it out, "The newspapers of national distribution, in addition to the general functions of every press organ, will serve as channels of expression of the aspirations, necessities, appreciations, criticisms and points of view of their respective sectors and of the entities and organisms which make them up."

Where did the Peruvian junta get the idea for such a press law? To counter hostile foreign opinion, the Embassy of Peru in the United States took out an advertisement in the *New York Times* on July 28, 1974, that partially answered this question. The communique concluded: "UNESCO studies clearly show the control that small minorities guided by economic ambition can exert upon the masses. The action of the Peruvian Government was designed to correct this unjust situation."

This touched a raw nerve with some U.S. publishers who had been viewing with alarm the efforts by UNESCO to establish national "communications policies" in the Third World since the sixteenth session of the General Conference of UNESCO in Paris in 1970. First targeted for discussion of readjustments between government and the press in underdeveloped nations was Latin America. A conference was held at San José, Costa Rica, on July 12–21, 1976, which seemed to endorse the action already taken by the Peruvian government. One article of the Declaration of San José, for example, stated, "There are sectors of the population which have yet to emerge from the isolation in which they live and [should] be helped to communicate with one another and to be informed about national and world-wide affairs."

This was certainly true of Peru, where the mass of Quechua-speaking *campesinos* are virtually excluded from national life. Further action on the UNESCO-proposed remedies was postponed for two years at a subsequent meeting in Nairobi, but it seemed clear that many emerging nations of the Third World were not hesitant to turn to governmental ownership or control of the means of communication if that would speed social and economic development.

Central to the UNESCO proposals to overcome underdevelopment was the creation of national or regional news agencies to provide a "balanced flow of news" rather than the largely one-way "free flow of news" coming from the industrialized countries to the Third World. Actually, this idea did not originate with UNESCO planners. As early as 1959, Pope John XXIII declared that the capitalist press could not cover the underdeveloped countries without bias. Therefore he urged the formation of regional news agencies organized as cooperatives.

Distrust of the well-established Western news agencies was long-standing in Peru. At a news conference in Santiago de Chile in 1946, for example, the Peruvian Aprista exiles Luis Alberto Sánchez and Manuel Seone declared, "Information from the news agencies cannot be taken very seriously." They cited the case of *El Comercio* of Lima, which had always supported oligarchical rule in Peru. The editor of *El Comercio*, they pointed out, was also the head of the Associated Press bureau in Lima; his brother headed the United Press bureau, and the editor of the afternoon edition of *El Comercio* was also responsible for the Reuters agency. It is scarcely any wonder that this ingrown and monopolistic situation prompted demands for national and international news services after the Peruvian revolution began in 1968.

Thus Peru moved not only to expropriate the eight leading dailies of Lima but also to establish a state-operated information-dispensing system. There they were not operating without precedent, for revolutionary Cuba had launched the Third World's first international news agency, *Prensa Latina*, in June 1959. Again, in 1970, thirteen leading Latin American newspapers pooled resources to form LATIN, a Latin American regional news agency with help from Reuters, one of the world news agencies. Peru, however, believed that the complexities and diversities of the region called for national news systems.

Given this framework, how is the system of expropriated newspapers working? One fear, widely voiced after 1974, was that freedom of press would be completely wiped out in Peru. This has not been the case altogether. Immediately after the 1974 takeover of the newspapers, for example, they launched a campaign against police brutality and torture—a crusade which did not bring government interference. Again, in 1976 when the regime closed twelve weekly publications, *Expreso*, one of the newspapers given to the educational sector, did not hesitate to blast the action with impunity. In an editorial entitled "Freedom of Expression," editor Juan Jóse Vega declared:

> And [our attitude] is based also on the conviction that without interlocutors, without opposition, without criticism it is not possible to move ahead. The opinions of the adversary, even unbending and irreducible, can help better than the obsequiousness of a gorged and ineffectual bureaucracy that has not known enough to point out problems in time and that with its unpardonable faults has placed in danger the very security of the nation.

Although this is only one example, it hardly sounds like the voice of a suppressed and servile press. But perhaps the best source to present the other side of the Peruvian press law controversy is to go to the state-appointed editors themselves. Here are thumbnail summaries of interviews with all the editors of the expropriated newspapers, conducted in August 1976, which give their open and frank responses to the effectiveness of the Peruvian press law two years after it went into operation:

—*Alfonso Tealdo Simi, El Comercio*: There was no freedom of the press in Peru before the press law—only freedom of action for the entrepreneurs. Vast segments of public opinion had no *representation*. *El Comercio* is primarily an urban newspaper, but it has a national circulation—the largest in the country—and is therefore appropriate for the *campesino* sector. Each newspaper has a newsprint quota controlled by the government, but the circulation of *El Comercio* has gone up since the nationalization. The newspapers have not yet been turned over directly to their sectors because the latter must widen their representativeness, and there is also the economic factor that the newspapers should first put their own houses in order. Nevertheless, the president of the *consejo directivo* is a *campesino*, along with four others on the ten-person body. *El Campesino* is published as a mid-week supplement and the third page every day is given over to *campesino* news.

—*Luis Jaime Cisneros Vizquerra, La Prensa*: The press law is unique, but we are witnessing its defects. We still live in the impassioned first moments of the revolution. Socialization in an objective of the law, but one cannot divide the country into sectors; one cannot invent artificial divisions. Frankly, the workers do not read *La Prensa* yet, but this is a long range project: much more than two years is needed. At first there were firings of ideologically antagonistic workers, but now all streams of opinion are represented among *La Prensa* workers.

—*Yi Carrillo, Ultima Hora*: I don't think the law has been a failure, but it has had its difficulties. Transfer of the newspapers to the sectors has been postponed for the second time because they are not organized or representative.

The press has become politicized after the press law. All newspapers became uniform because of the imposition of ideology. I believe in liberty of the press and think the government should give greater latitude toward freedom of expression. But the public will be the judge of last resort; they will decide whether the press law is a good idea or not. In my view, ideas cannot be imposed; they must be contagious.

—*Juan José Vega, Expreso* and *Extra*: What the assignment of newspapers to sectors was designed to do was to overcome the social hatred between groups and classes which permeates our society. Each sector was to have a voice that would be heard in the national arena. As to charges made by *Miami Herald* correspondent William Montalbano that the largest union of teachers is not represented among the directors of *Expreso*, the unions do not represent the bases of the workers, and teachers are not the major part of the educational community. Nevertheless, teachers buy *Expreso* more than any other paper, and circulation has gone up 50 percent since the press law was enacted.

—*César Miró, Ojo*: Even though *Ojo* has been given to the cultural organizations, it is very popular and has the greatest circulation in the country. Luis Banchero Rossi, a fishing magnate killed in 1972, founded the newspaper chain of *Correo* (1962) which once had five newspapers of that name in Peru, and *Ojo* (1968). Newsprint is our biggest problem because that imported from Canada is now 30,000 soles a ton, whereas it used to be 20,000. All newspapers have weekly supplements for their sectors. Most importantly, the press law is necessary for the social changes now underway in Peru.

—*Antenor del Pozo, Correo*: The press law of 1974 has been a great success. Before then, there was no representation of the needs or aspirations of the workers or *campesinos*. Now newspapers are to serve the interests of the sectors—ours is the professional organizations—without harming their coverage of the general community. Transfer of the newspapers to their sectors has been postponed twice because the representation of the sectors is not broad enough, and indemnization must be carried through first.

—*Jose Luis Brousset Escobar, La Cronica* and *Tercera*: Has the press law been a success or failure? One cannot categorize. The press law cannot be automatically imposed, but on the other hand there was the previous danger of an excess of power in the hands of the [newspaper] entrepreneurs. As for the closing of twelve magazines two months ago, there cannot be liberty of subversion. *La Crónica* and *Tercera* are official spokesmen; what they and the sector newspapers are trying to do is provide the equilibrium—a balancing of forces—so desperately needed in Peruvian society.

These voices from Peru reflect in a few instances the doubt and skepticism which many outside observers feel about the practicality of the Peruvian press law of 1974. But it is significant that they are not merely pale echoes of the government's position. What seems to be happening is that a *modus operandi* is evolving between the state-appointed editors and the government itself. To illustrate this, in the first two years of the law's operation, the whole slate of editors was changed three separate times. In the third postponement of turning the newspapers over to their sectors on July 27, 1977, however, only one editor was replaced. He was José Luis Brousset Escóbar of *La Crónica*, the only one of the seven editors interviewed who had had no previous journalism experience. At the beginning, some observers feared that only government syncophants or dilettantes would be named to the posts of editors, but this has not been the case. Most were chosen for their long services to the newspapers concerned. Brousset, president of Banco Popular, the second largest bank in Peru, was an exception, but he has been replaced as editor of *La Crónica* by Carlos Quiroga.

In conclusion, it is freely conceded that only one side of the coin has been presented in this paper, but it is a side which has been largely ignored to date. Several observations present themselves:

- Peruvians facing Peruvian realities should be free to search for Peruvian solutions without facing harassment by a frequently uninformed and hostile world press.
- Much more time is needed to determine whether the Peruvian press law is indeed workable. Many Peruvian intellectuals favor it, but there are distinguished exceptions, such as novelist Mario Vargas Llosa.
- "Freedom of the Press" means different things to different people. One study concluded that the IAPA in the case of the Bolivian National Revolution for example, seemed to be more interested in protecting property rights than freedom of expression.
- Control of the press may be necessary in a society undergoing profound transformation. We experienced it in the U.S. during our Civil War when the issues were mainly political and military. It is much more difficult in a social revolution when the issues are social and economic, and the enemy is less visible.

The last two points are perhaps the most significant ones to draw from this brief examination of the Peruvian press law of 1974. Some of us in the United States and Western Europe tend to forget that the Peruvian culture is radically different from our own. As one small indication of this, there are no words in the Quechua language, spoken by the large bulk of Peruvian Indians, for "newspaper" or "to read," since their Incan forebears had no written means of expression. What then does an abstract concept such as "freedom of the press" mean to such people? They are interested in more adequate food for their families, better shelter and clothing, schools and medical care.

"Freedom of the press" as practiced in Lima by the Miró Quesadas and Beltráns and others did not free these *campesinos* from their rural and psychological isolation. Now they have a newspaper, *El Comercio*, the largest and oldest in Peru. True, most cannot read it and many who can read still do not have access to it, but they do have a newspaper. It is an enormous symbolic advance which perhaps time will give substantial meaning. As A.J. Liebling, the late *New Yorker* press critic, once wrote, "Freedom of the press belongs to those who can afford one." In Peru, there are few persons who can afford a printing press, and the government is trying to redress that imbalance.

A POSTSCRIPT

As this article was going to press, the Peruvian government acted on July 18 to divest itself of the newspapers discussed here, almost exactly four years after the Peruvian press law was adopted. Under the new decree issued by right-leaning President Francisco Morales Bermúdez, after one year press workers will have the opportunity to buy 25 percent of the newspaper shares, with state financial aid; the former owners, another 25 percent, and the remaining 50 percent will be sold to anyone on the stock exchange. The compromise has pleased no one, however, and the issue may be tossed in the lap of Peru's newly elected constituent assembly.

(Jerry W. Knudson. "The Peruvian Press Law of 1974: The Other Side of the Coin," *Mass Comm Review*, 5:2 (Spring 1978), 7–13.)

www.ingramcontent.com/pod-product-compliance
Lightning Source LLC
Chambersburg PA
CBHW050527270326
41926CB00015B/3101